Square Tile Explorations and Problems

Don Miller & Bishnu Naraine
St. Cloud State University

TRICON Publishing
Mt. Pleasant, Michigan

Printed in the United States

ISBN 1-883547-08-3

CONTENTS

SECTION 1: Number Tiles

Circle Puzzle	1
Triangle Puzzle	2
Crossing Tile Puzzle	3
Magic Square (3x3)	4
One's Digit Challenges	5
2x2 Puzzles	6
Addition Games (2x2, 2x3, 3x3)	7-9
Addition Puzzles (2x3)	10-12
Puzzles (2x3)	13-15
Addition Challenges (3x3)	16-18
Missing Digit Challenges	19-20
Guess Operations (2x3)	21
3 Equations (3x3)	22-27
Puzzles (3x3)	28-31
6 Equations (3x3)	32-33
5-Minute Challenges	34-37
Equations Challenges	38-39
5-Target Challenges	40-41
Tic-Tac-Toe	42-45
7-Digit Challenges	46
4 in-a-line	47
Target Problems	48-52
Addition Challenges	53-54
Subtraction Challenges	55-56
Mixed Challenges	57
Digit Challenges	58
Estimation:	
Missing Digits	59-60
Mental Math	61-65
Game	66
Skills	67
Square Roots	68
Percents	69
Number Theory:	
Probability Challenges	70
6-Digit Challenges	71
Missing Digits	72
Sums and Products	73
Sets	74-77

SECTION 2: Square Tiles

Sets and Subsets	78
True? or False?	79
Red and Blue Tiles	80
U-shaped Arrangements	81
Counting Border Squares	82-83
Factors and Square Tiles	84
Rectangles and Fractions	85
Perimeter and Square Tiles	86
Area and Square Tiles	87
4x4 Square Challenges	88
Color Tile Clues	89
Pentominoes	90
Reflections	91
Your Color Tile Patterns	92-94
Color Tile Patterns	95
About How Many Tiles?	96
Puzzles and Games:	
Jumping Tiles	97
Tower Puzzle	98
2 in-a-line	99
Try-To-Switch	100
Tiles Game	101
3 in-a-line	102
2-player game	103
Color Tiles in-a-line	104
Last Player Loses	105
Dice Coverup	106
3-D Tic-Tac-Toe	107
3-Player Tic-Tac-Toe	108
Rectangular Patterns	109
Answers	110-116

Introduction

The purpose of this book is to provide teachers with a ready source of activities which show how numbered or colored square tiles can be used to introduce and/or reinforce a variety of mathematical ideas via non-routine problem situations. Some of the activities are designed to help students improve their mental and estimation skills, some challenge students via equations or familiar computational algorithms, some use the tiles to introduce geometric ideas, some are strategy games, and some involve open-ended problems. The main goal for all of the activities is to provide students with experiences designed to improve their mathematical skills while also helping them to become better problem solvers.

Most of the activities have been used successfully in classes and/or workshops for elementary and middle school teachers, and later with students in their respective classrooms. It is because of their many positive comments that we decided to write this book. It should also be noted that many pages were designed to serve as transparency masters. These may be used to enhance whole class discussion and eliminate the need to duplicate the activity for each student.

The mathematical content in this book spans a wide age and ability range. The book is particularly suitable for grades 4-9, as well as for pre-service and in-service teacher training courses and workshops. The pages need not be done in sequence or in total. For use in the classroom, teachers should consider student backgrounds before selecting activities which may be appropriate either to introduce new mathematical ideas or to reinforce previously developed concepts.

The materials listed below will be needed to complete the activities in this book. The nine numbered tiles will be used in the first part of the book. One way to number the tiles is to use stick-on circles. The 24 colored tiles will be needed for the remaining activities. Based on teacher recommendations, maximum results will be realized only if each student has the tiles suggested for each activity, even when they are working together in small groups.

Materials:

Nine square numbered tiles:

24 square colored tiles: 6 red   6 blue   6 yellow   6 green

Place the numbered tiles (1-9) into the squares so that each "diameter" has a sum of 15.

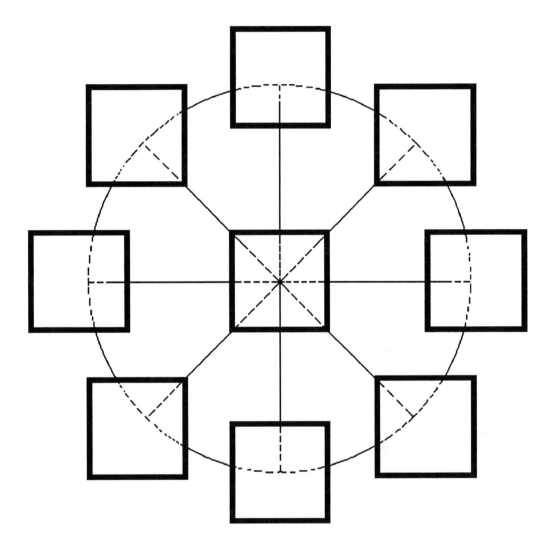

*Show why the center number cannot be 8.

Place the tiles (1-9) so that the total of the numbers on each side of the triangle is the same. Is there more than one solution?

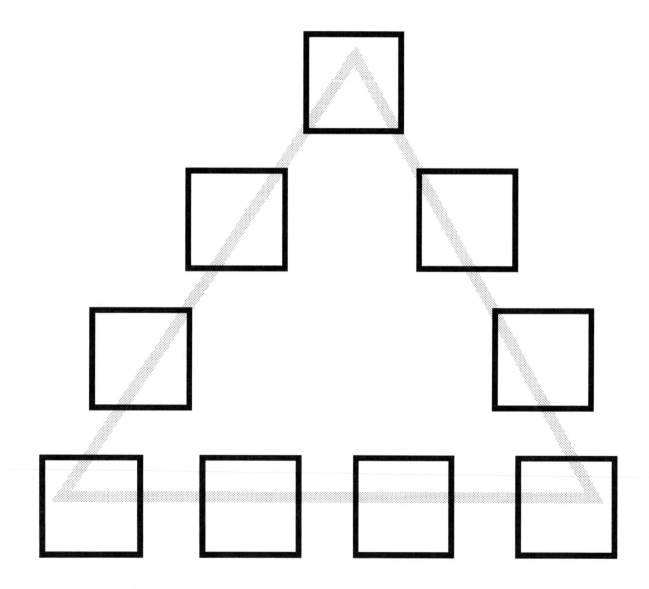

 Square Tile Explorations and Problems

Place the numbered tiles into the nine squares so that the sum vertically and horizontally is:

a. 23   b. 24   c. 25   d. 26.

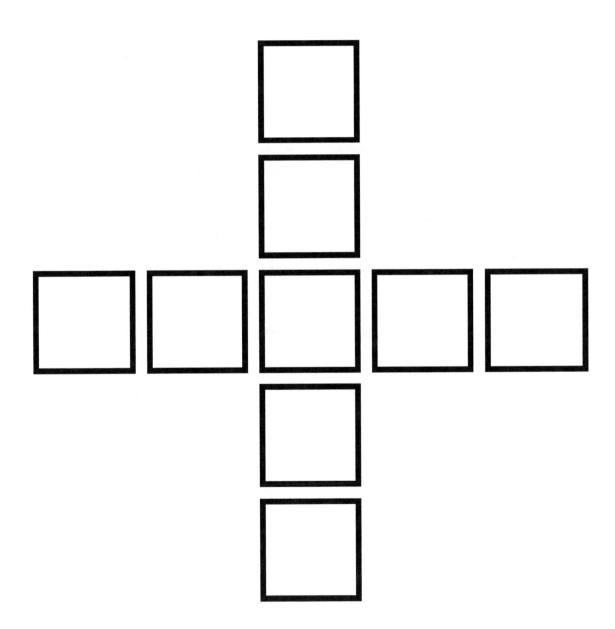

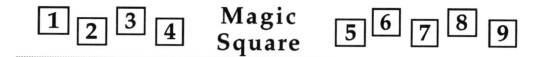

The number squares shown above can be arranged in a 3 by 3 array so that each row, column, and diagonal has the same sum (magic square).

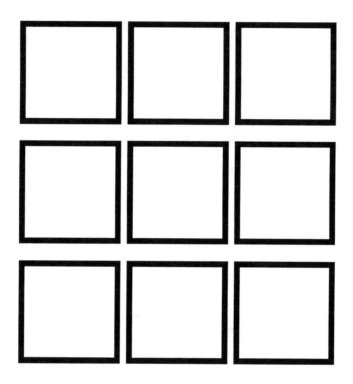

1. Show why the center number must be 5.

2. Show why 1 cannot be a corner number.

3. Show why the corner numbers cannot all be odd.

4. Form a magic square by placing the 9 numbered tiles.

5. Challenge:
    Try to place the 9 numbered tiles so that the sum in each row, column, and diagonal is different (Un-Magic Square).

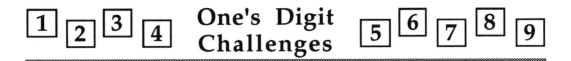
Randomly select one of the numbered tiles. That number is the "Target Digit." Then try to place the remaining 8 digits on the board so that the sums of the two rows (A+B+C, F+G+H) and the sums of the two columns (A+D+F, C+E+H) end with the "Target Digit."

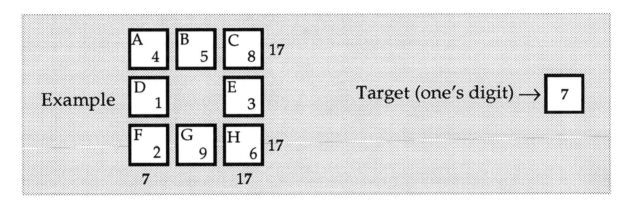

Example

A	B	C	
4	5	8	17

D		E	
1		3	

F	G	H	
2	9	6	17

7   17

Target (one's digit) → 7

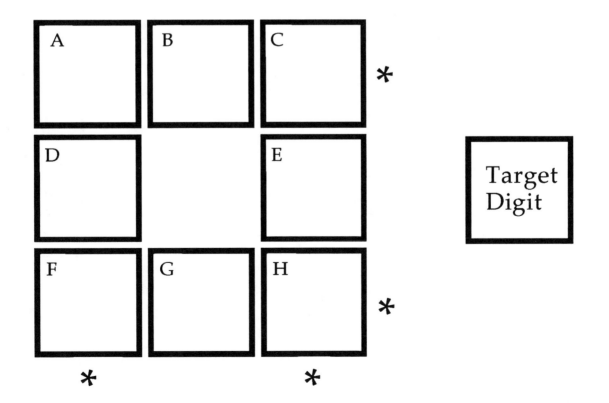

Target Digit

Try to find the missing numbers. Each empty square represents a different digit.

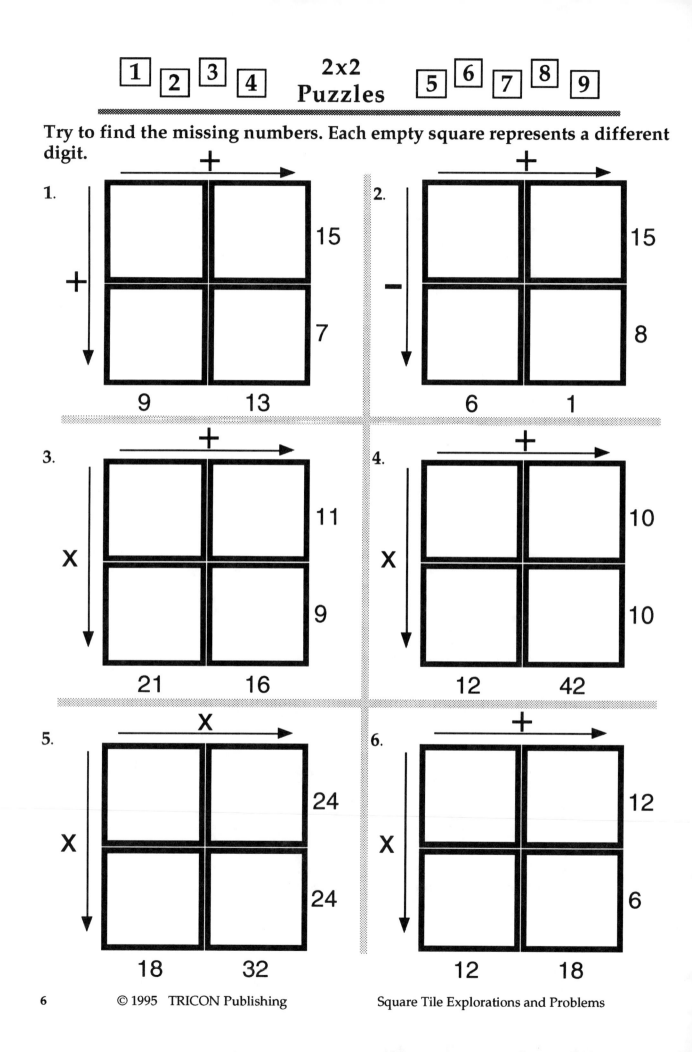

1.
+
15
7
9   13

2.
+
−
15
8
6   1

3.
+
X
11
9
21   16

4.
+
X
10
10
12   42

5.
X
X
24
24
18   32

6.
+
X
12
6
12   18

     Square Tile Explorations and Problems

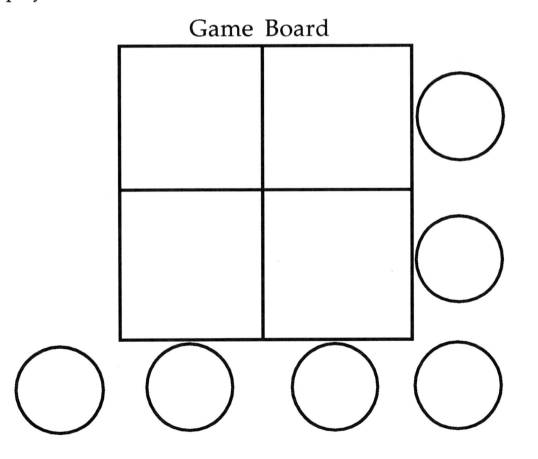

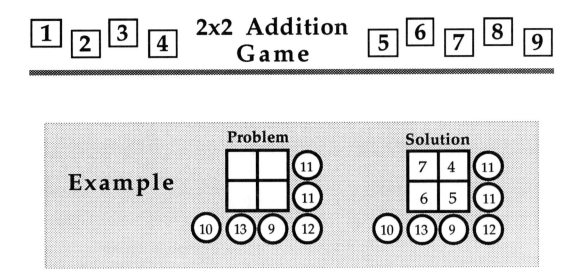

2x2 Addition Game

Example

Problem

Solution

*Study the given example.
*Materials: Nine # tiles (1-9) and 1 Game Board for each player.
*2-4 players each make up a **problem** on their game board.
*In turn, the players then display their game board.
*Each of the other players scores 1 point for a correct **solution**.
*Continue until exactly one player scores at least 3 points.
*That player wins the game when he/she has more points than the other players.

Game Board

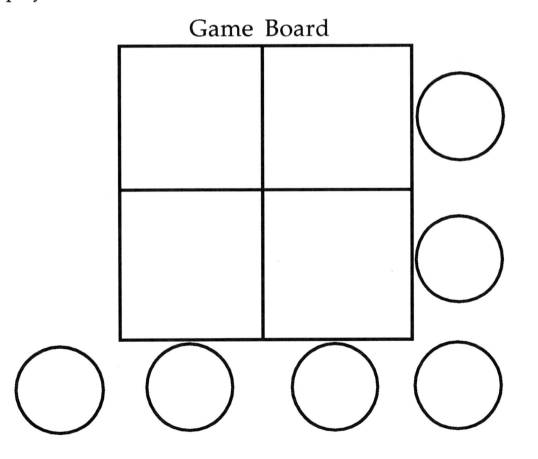

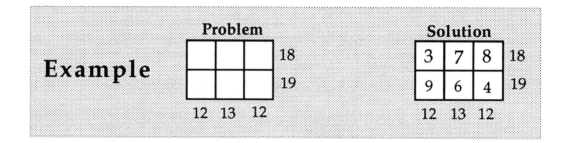

2x3 Addition Game

Example

Problem

			18
			19

12 13 12

Solution

3	7	8	18
9	6	4	19

12 13 12

*Study the given example.
*Materials: Nine # tiles (1-9) and 1 Game Board for each player.
*2-4 players each make up a **problem** on their game board.
*In turn, the players then display their game board.
*Each of the other players scores 1 point for a correct **solution**.
*Continue until exactly one player scores at least 3 points.
*That player wins the game when he/she has more points than the other players.

Game Board

			____
			____

____   ____   ____

              Square Tile Explorations and Problems

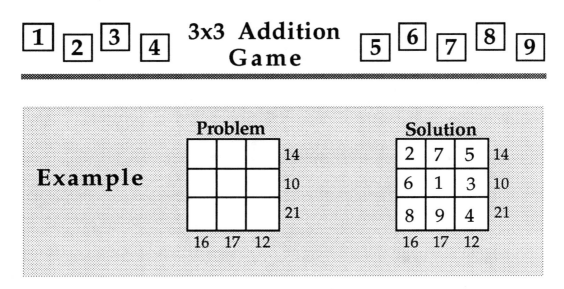

Example

Problem			
			14
			10
			21
16	17	12	

Solution			
2	7	5	14
6	1	3	10
8	9	4	21
16	17	12	

*Study the given example.

*Materials: Nine # tiles (1-9) and 1 Game Board for each player.

*2-4 players each make up a **problem** on their game board.

*In turn, the players then display their game board.

*Each of the other players scores 1 point for a correct **solution**.

*Continue until exactly one player scores at least 3 points.

*That player wins the game when he/she has more points than the other players.

Game Board

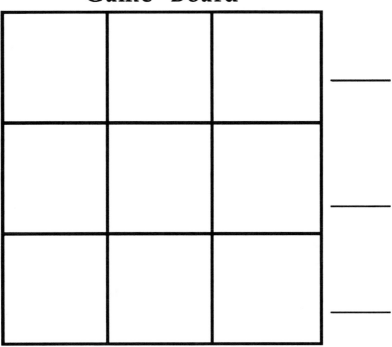

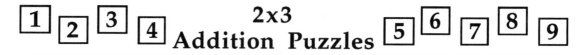
Try to find the missing numbers. Each empty square represents a different digit.

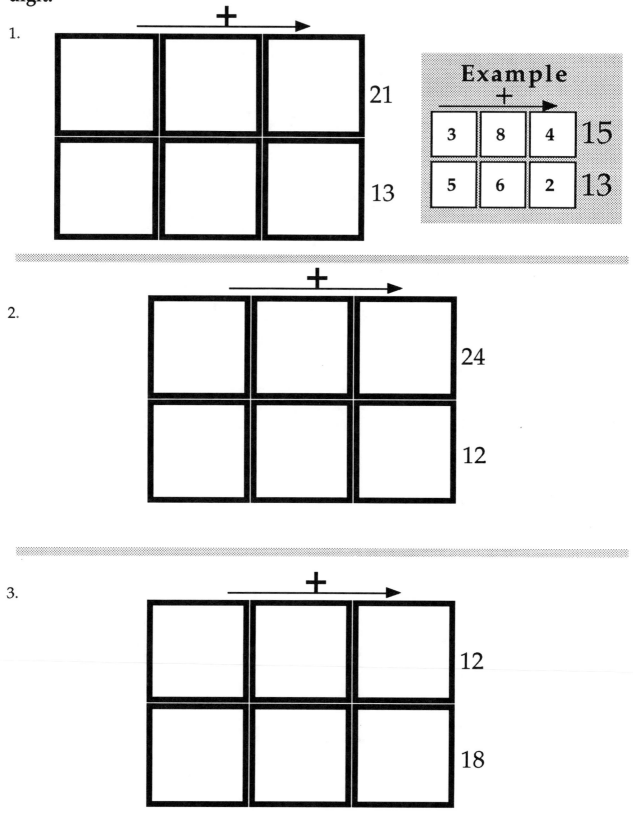

1.

21

13

Example

| 3 | 8 | 4 | 15 |
| 5 | 6 | 2 | 13 |

2.

24

12

3.

12

18

Try to find the missing numbers. Each empty square represents a different digit.

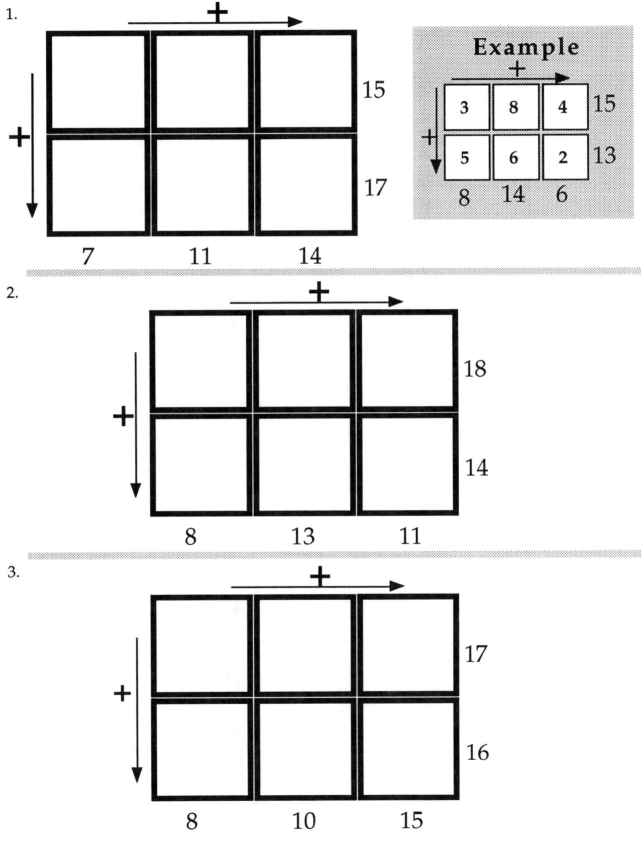

1.

			15
			17
7	11	14	

Example

3	8	4	15
5	6	2	13
8	14	6	

2.

			18
			14
8	13	11	

3.

			17
			16
8	10	15	

Try to find the missing numbers. Each empty square represents a different digit.

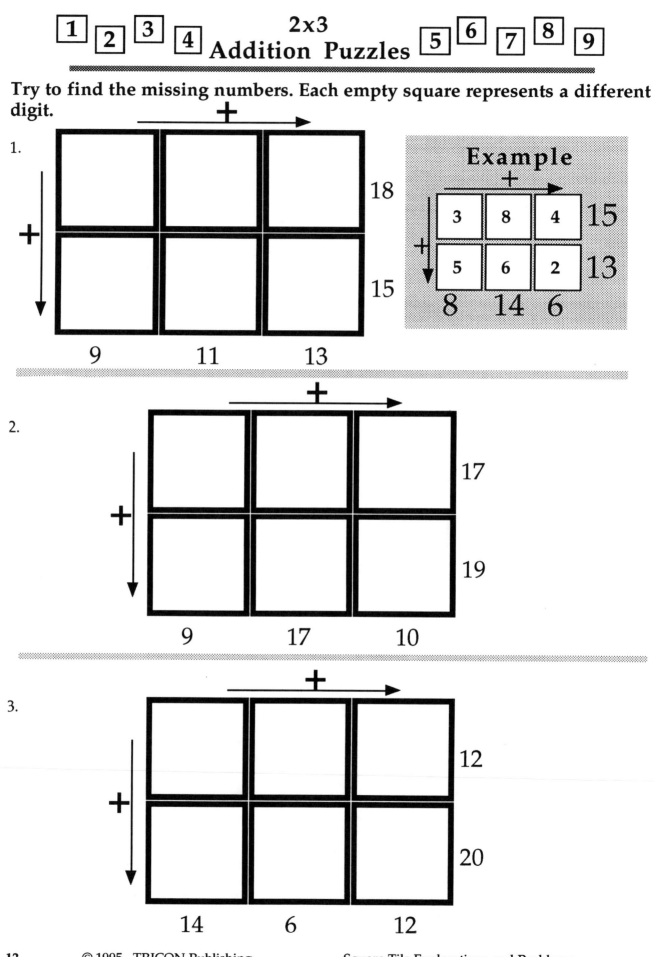

1.

+ →

| | | | 18 |
| | | | 15 |

9   11   13

Example

+ →

| 3 | 8 | 4 | 15 |
| 5 | 6 | 2 | 13 |

8   14   6

2.

+ →

| | | | 17 |
| | | | 19 |

9   17   10

3.

+ →

| | | | 12 |
| | | | 20 |

14   6   12

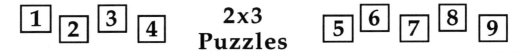

Try to find the missing numbers. Each empty square represents a different digit.

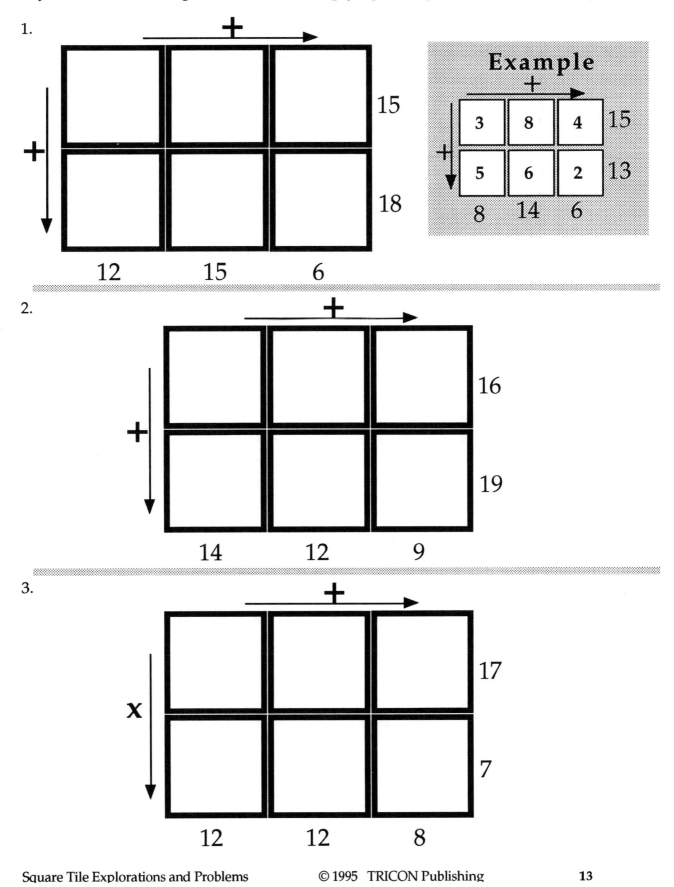

1.

			+ →
			15
			18
12	15	6	

Example

+ →

3	8	4	15
5	6	2	13
8	14	6	

2.

			+ →
			16
			19
14	12	9	

3.

			+ →
			17
			7
12	12	8	

X (down arrow on left of puzzle 3)

Try to find the missing numbers. Each empty square represents a different digit.

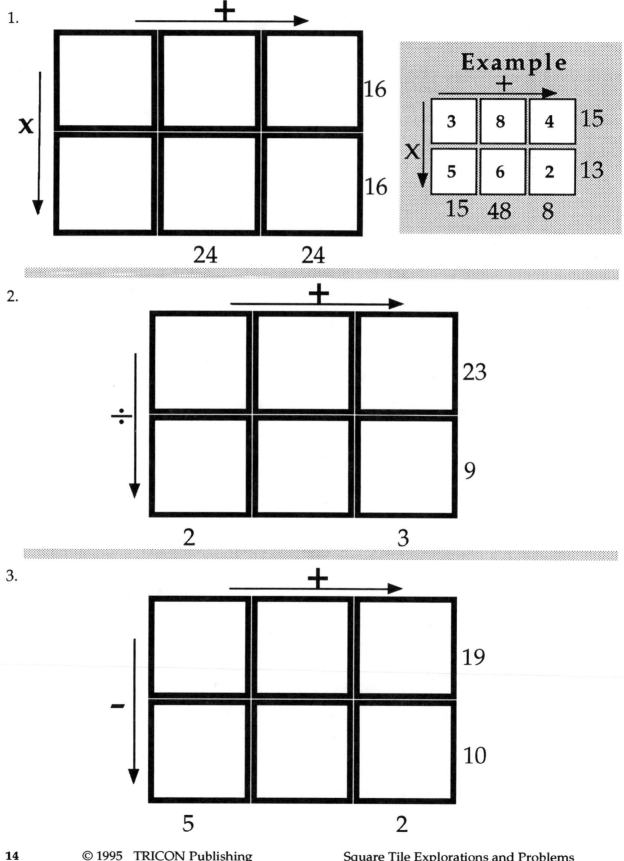

1.

+

| | | | 16 |
| | | | 16 |

X

24   24

Example

+

| 3 | 8 | 4 | 15 |
| 5 | 6 | 2 | 13 |

X

15 48 8

2.

+

| | | | 23 |
| | | | 9 |

÷

2   3

3.

+

| | | | 19 |
| | | | 10 |

−

5   2

Square Tile Explorations and Problems

Try to find the missing numbers. Each empty square represents a different digit.

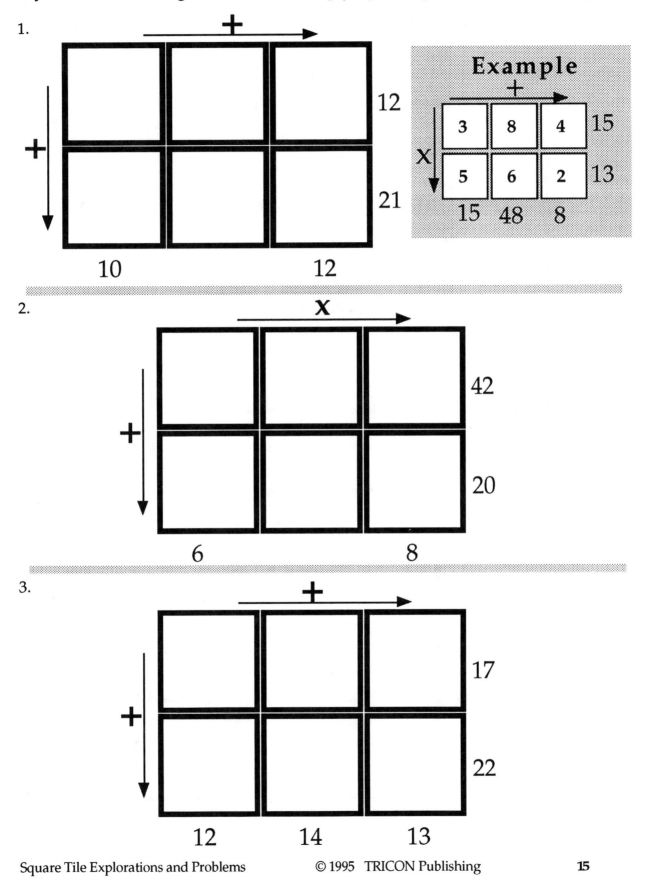

1.

12

21

10   12

Example

| 3 | 8 | 4 | 15 |
| 5 | 6 | 2 | 13 |

15 48 8

2.

42

20

6   8

3.

17

22

12   14   13

Find the missing numbers. Each empty square represents a different digit.

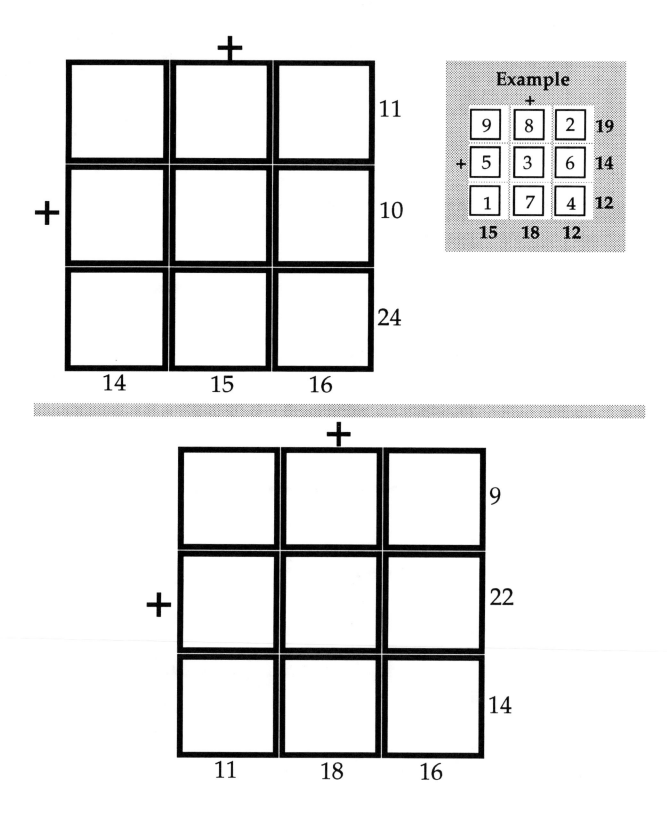

Example
+

9	8	2	**19**
+ 5	3	6	**14**
1	7	4	**12**
15	**18**	**12**	

Find the missing numbers. Each empty square represents a different digit.

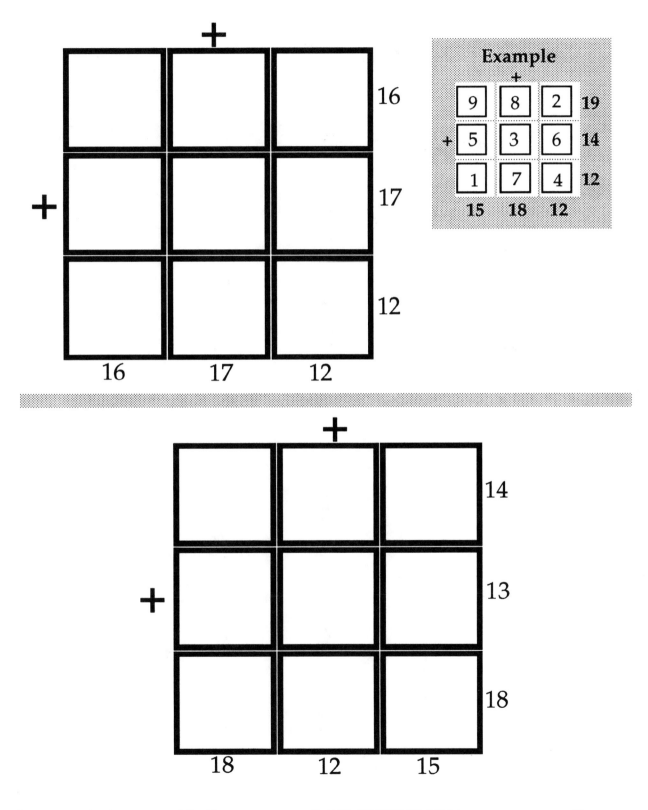

Example
+

9	8	2	19
5	3	6	14
1	7	4	12
15	18	12	

Find the missing numbers. Each empty square represents a different digit.

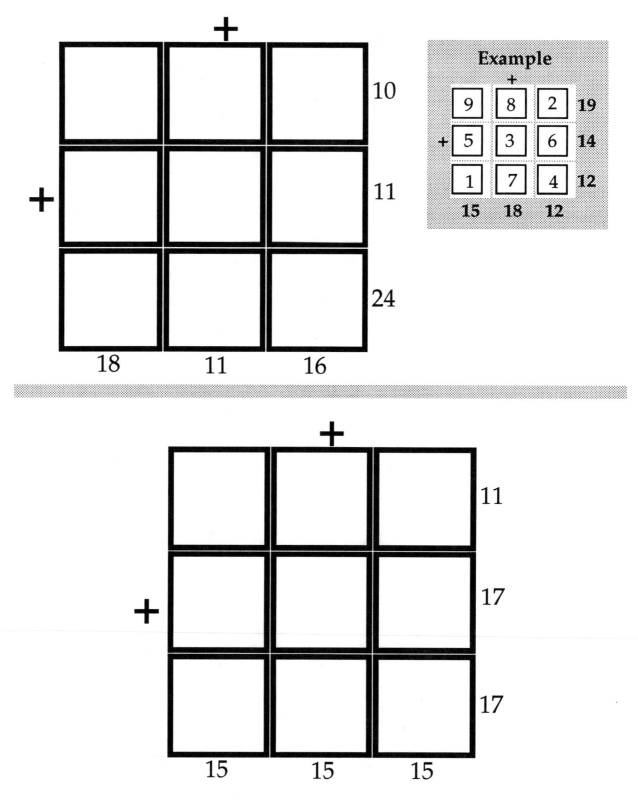

Example
+

9	8	2	19
5	3	6	14
1	7	4	12
15	18	12	

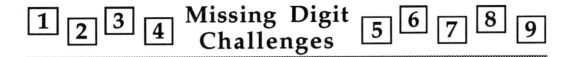
Study the given example. Then try to use the numbered tiles (1-9) to help you complete the below problems in the same way.

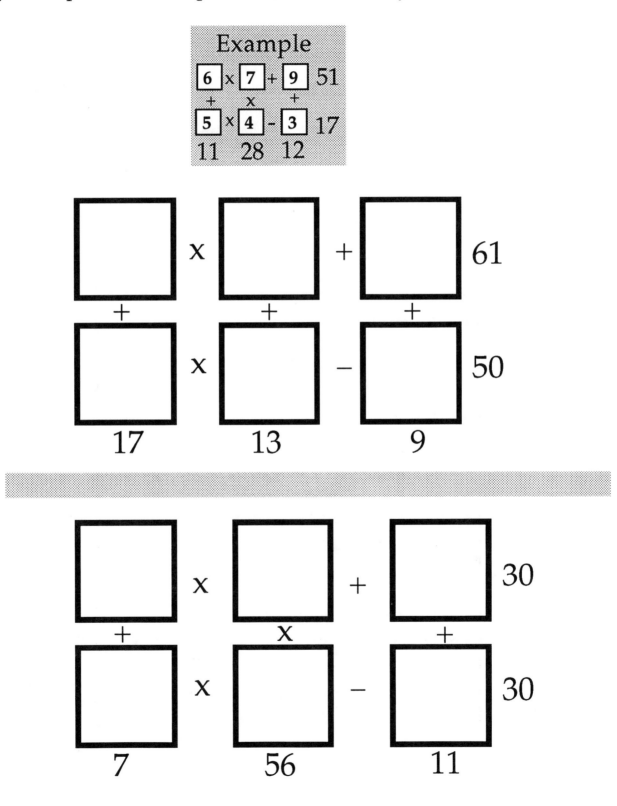

Missing Digit Challenges

Study the given example. Then try to use the numbered tiles (1-9) to help you complete the below problems in the same way.

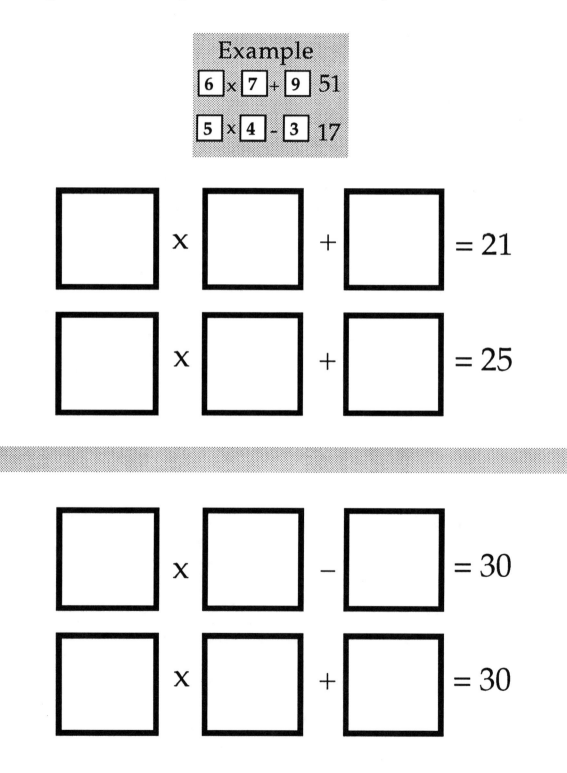

Square Tile Explorations and Problems

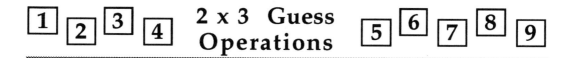

2 x 3 Guess Operations

Study the examples. Then, in this way, try to use six of the nine tiles (1-9) to form two true equations where the answers are the given numbers A and B. Record your solutions.

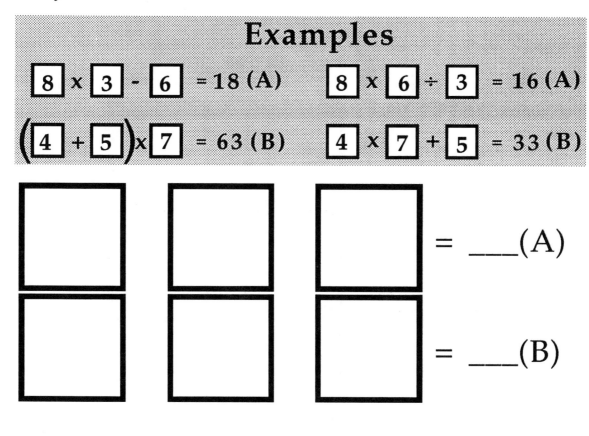

1. A = 38   B = 21

2. A = 70   B = 29

3. A = 71   B = 44

4. A = 36   B = 30

5. A = 47   B = 23

6. A = 12   B = 60

7. A = 17   B = 30

8. A = 20   B = 21

9. A = 47   B = 21

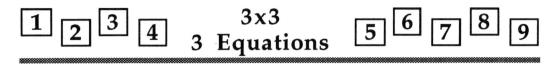
Try to place the numbered tiles (1-9) into the squares so that each statement ends up as a true equation.

Example
$$4 \times 3 - 5 = 7$$
$$(6 - 2) \times 9 = 36$$
$$7 \times 8 - 1 = 55$$

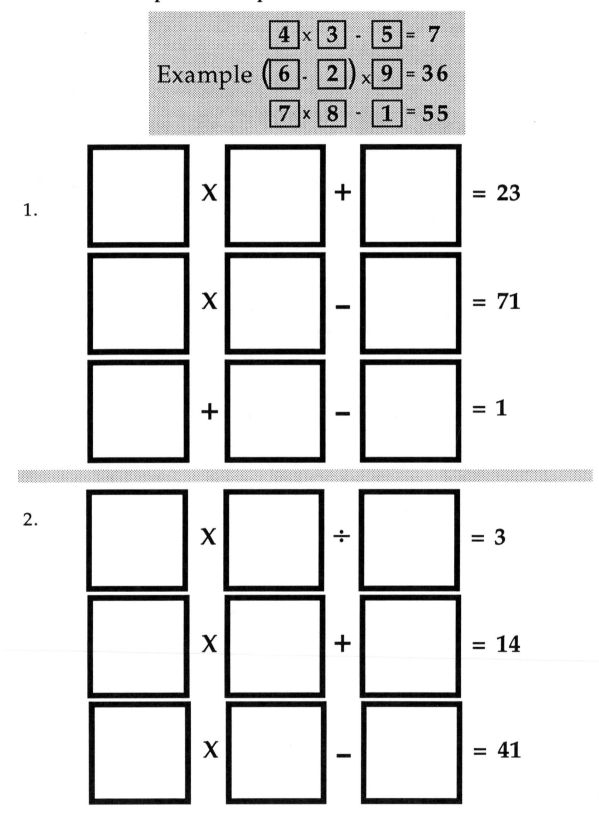

1.
$$\square \times \square + \square = 23$$
$$\square \times \square - \square = 71$$
$$\square + \square - \square = 1$$

2.
$$\square \times \square \div \square = 3$$
$$\square \times \square + \square = 14$$
$$\square \times \square - \square = 41$$

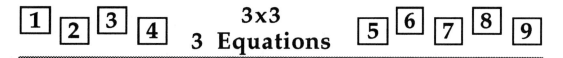
Try to place the numbered tiles (1-9) into the squares so that each statement ends up as a true equation.

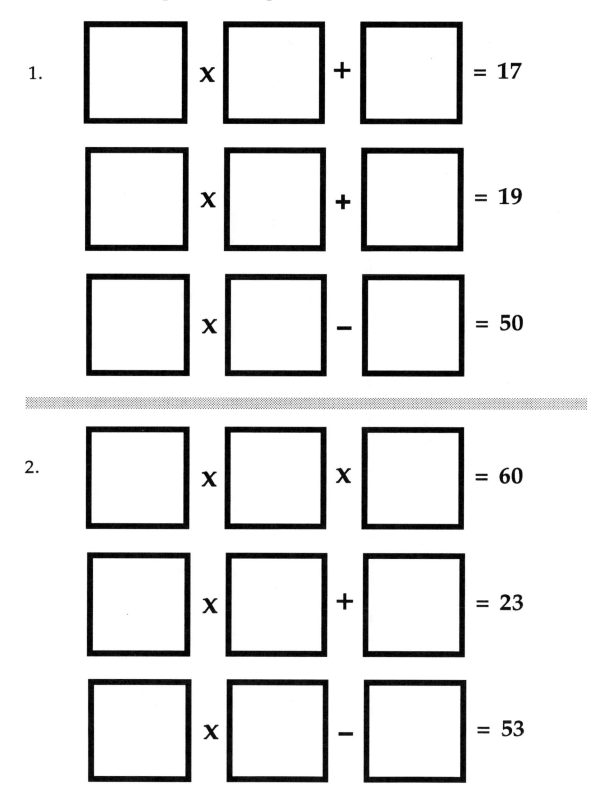

1.

☐ X ☐ + ☐ = 17

☐ X ☐ + ☐ = 19

☐ X ☐ - ☐ = 50

2.

☐ X ☐ X ☐ = 60

☐ X ☐ + ☐ = 23

☐ X ☐ - ☐ = 53

Try to place the numbered tiles (1-9) into the squares so that each statement ends up as a true equation.

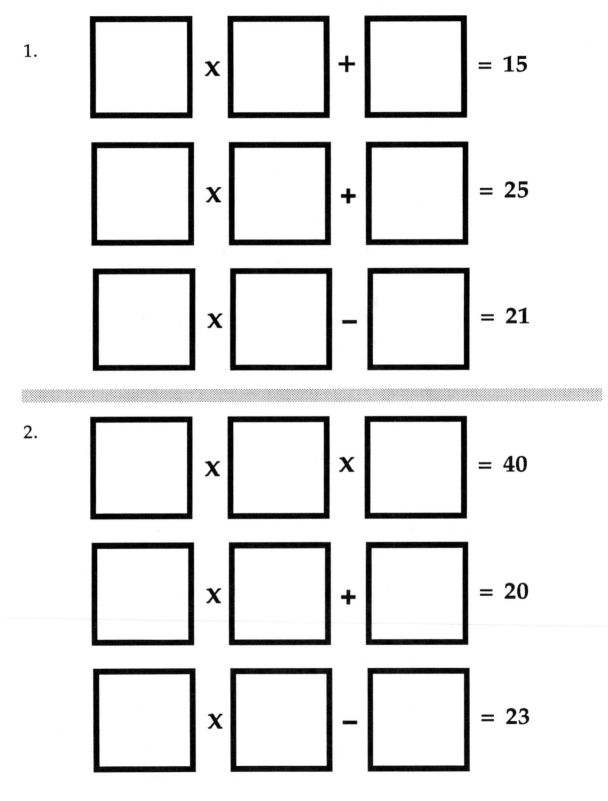

1. ☐ X ☐ + ☐ = 15

   ☐ X ☐ + ☐ = 25

   ☐ X ☐ − ☐ = 21

2. ☐ X ☐ X ☐ = 40

   ☐ X ☐ + ☐ = 20

   ☐ X ☐ − ☐ = 23

Square Tile Explorations and Problems

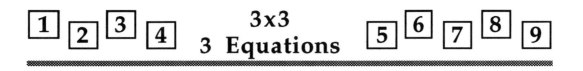
Try to place the numbered tiles (1-9) into the squares so that each statement ends up as a true equation.

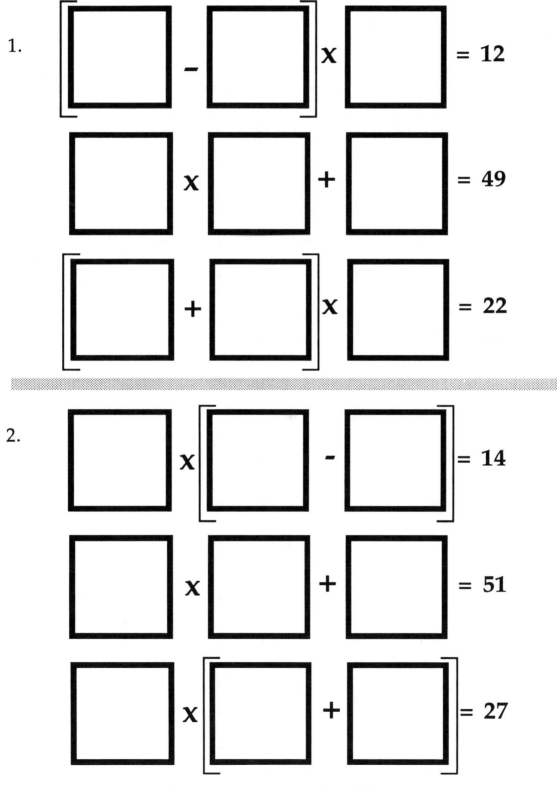

1.

$[\ \square - \square\ ] \times \square = 12$

$\square \times \square + \square = 49$

$[\ \square + \square\ ] \times \square = 22$

2.

$\square \times [\ \square - \square\ ] = 14$

$\square \times \square + \square = 51$

$\square \times [\ \square + \square\ ] = 27$

Try to place the numbered tiles (1-9) into the squares so that each statement ends up as a true equation.

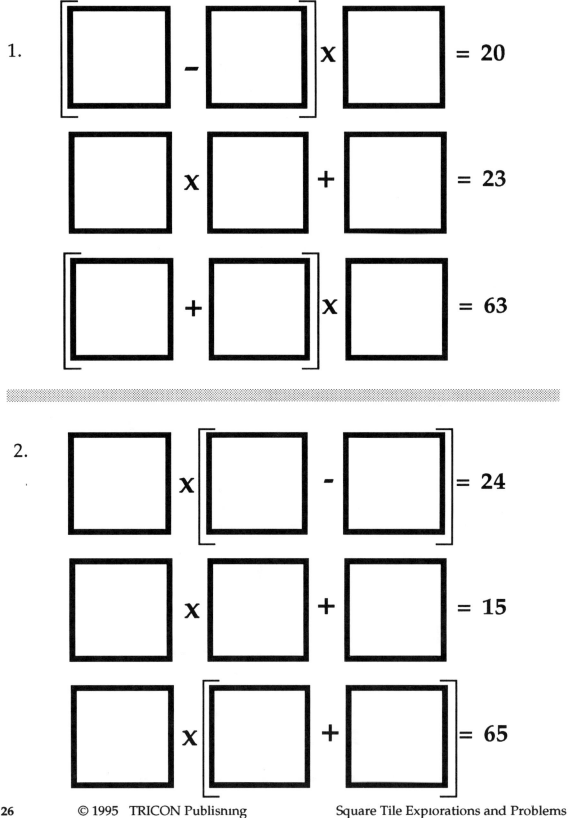

1.

$$[\Box - \Box] \times \Box = 20$$

$$\Box \times \Box + \Box = 23$$

$$[\Box + \Box] \times \Box = 63$$

2.

$$\Box \times [\Box - \Box] = 24$$

$$\Box \times \Box + \Box = 15$$

$$\Box \times [\Box + \Box] = 65$$

Square Tile Explorations and Problems

Try to place the numbered tiles (1-9) into the squares so that each statement ends up as a true equation.

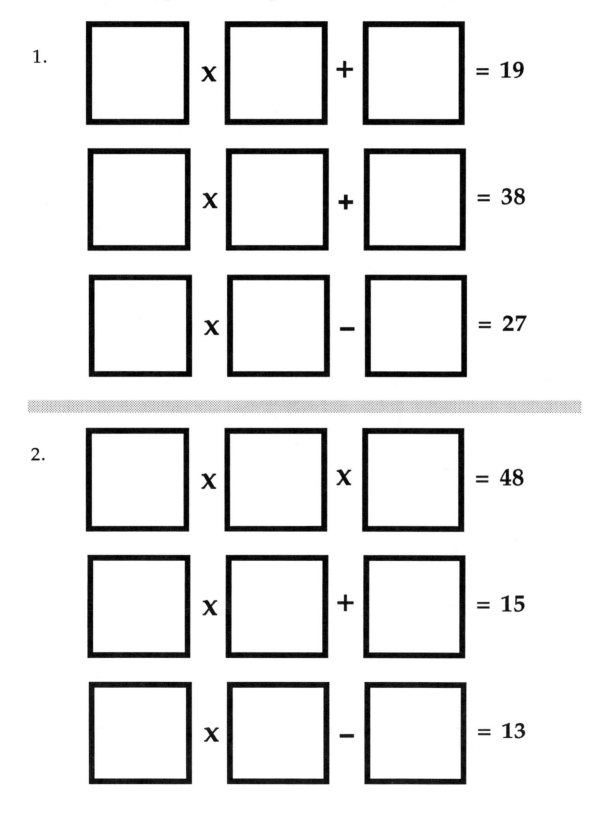

1. ☐ X ☐ + ☐ = 19

   ☐ X ☐ + ☐ = 38

   ☐ X ☐ − ☐ = 27

2. ☐ X ☐ X ☐ = 48

   ☐ X ☐ + ☐ = 15

   ☐ X ☐ − ☐ = 13

Study the examples. Then, in this way, try to use the nine tiles (1-9) to form three true equations where the answers are the given numbers A, B, & C. Record your solutions.

Examples: 4x6-2=22(A)   7(9-3)=42(B)   1x5x8=40(C)

2x3x7=42(A)   8(4+5)=72(B)   6x9+1=55(C)

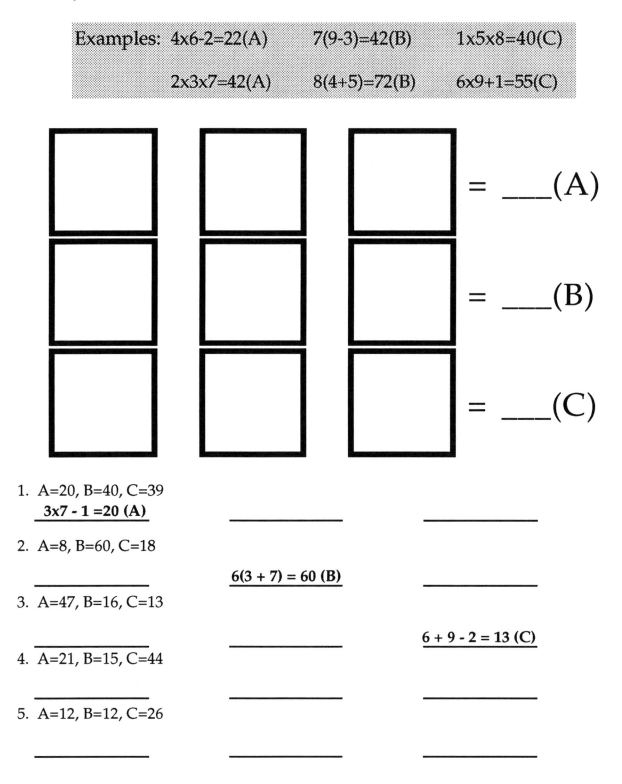

= ___(A)

= ___(B)

= ___(C)

1. A=20, B=40, C=39
   <u>3x7 - 1 =20 (A)</u>   _____   _____

2. A=8, B=60, C=18
                    <u>6(3 + 7) = 60 (B)</u>   _____

3. A=47, B=16, C=13
   _____   _____   <u>6 + 9 - 2 = 13 (C)</u>

4. A=21, B=15, C=44
   _____   _____   _____

5. A=12, B=12, C=26
   _____   _____   _____

Square Tile Explorations and Problems

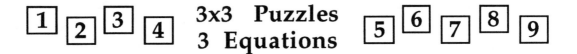

Study the examples. Then, in this way, try to use the nine tiles (1-9) to form three true equations where the answers are the given numbers A, B, & C. Record your solutions.

Examples: 4x6-2=22(A)   7(9-3)=42(B)   1x5x8=40(C)

2x3x7=42(A)   8(4+5)=72(B)   6x9+1=55(C)

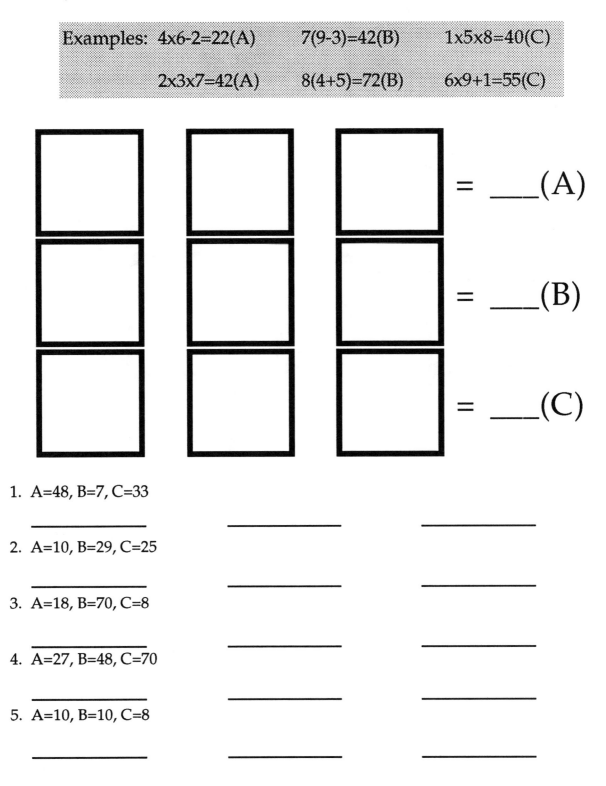

= ___(A)

= ___(B)

= ___(C)

1. A=48, B=7, C=33

_____   _____   _____

2. A=10, B=29, C=25

_____   _____   _____

3. A=18, B=70, C=8

_____   _____   _____

4. A=27, B=48, C=70

_____   _____   _____

5. A=10, B=10, C=8

_____   _____   _____

Study the examples. Then, in this way, try to use the nine tiles (1-9) to form three true equations where the answers are the given numbers A, B, & C. Record your solutions.

Examples: 4x6-2=22(A)   7(9-3)=42(B)   1x5x8=40(C)

2x3x7=42(A)   8(4+5)=72(B)   6x9+1=55(C)

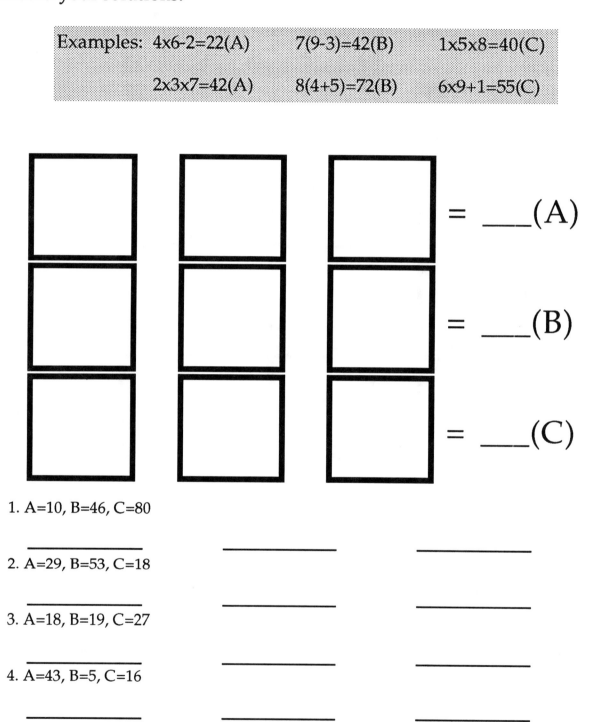

= ___(A)

= ___(B)

= ___(C)

1. A=10, B=46, C=80

_____   _____   _____

2. A=29, B=53, C=18

_____   _____   _____

3. A=18, B=19, C=27

_____   _____   _____

4. A=43, B=5, C=16

_____   _____   _____

5. A=18, B=32, C=81

_____   _____   _____

Square Tile Explorations and Problems

Study the examples. Then, in this way, try to use the nine tiles (1-9) to form three true equations where the answers are the given numbers A, B, & C. Record your solutions.

Examples: 4x6-2=22(A)   7(9-3)=42(B)   1x5x8=40(C)

2x3x7=42(A)   8(4+5)=72(B)   6x9+1=55(C)

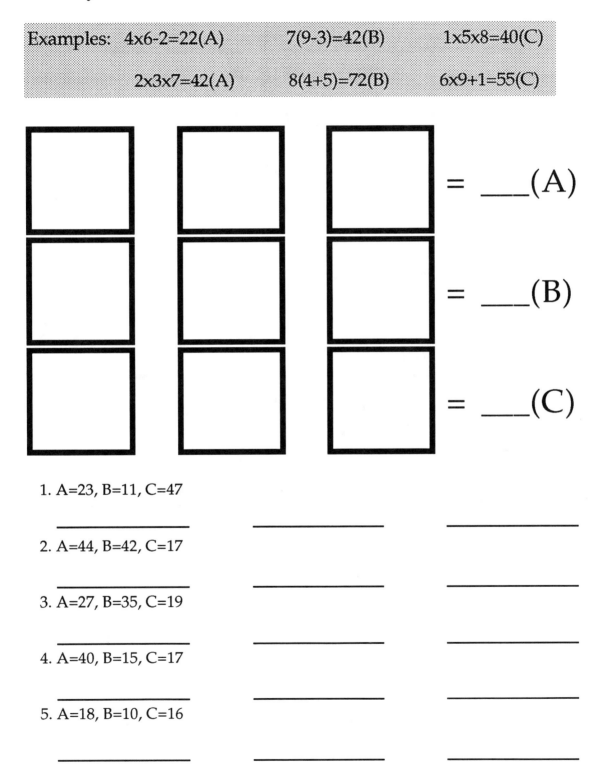

= ___(A)

= ___(B)

= ___(C)

1. A=23, B=11, C=47

_____   _____   _____

2. A=44, B=42, C=17

_____   _____   _____

3. A=27, B=35, C=19

_____   _____   _____

4. A=40, B=15, C=17

_____   _____   _____

5. A=18, B=10, C=16

_____   _____   _____

Study the given example. Then try to use the nine tiles to help you find the missing digits.

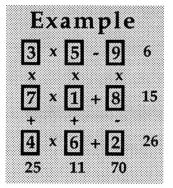

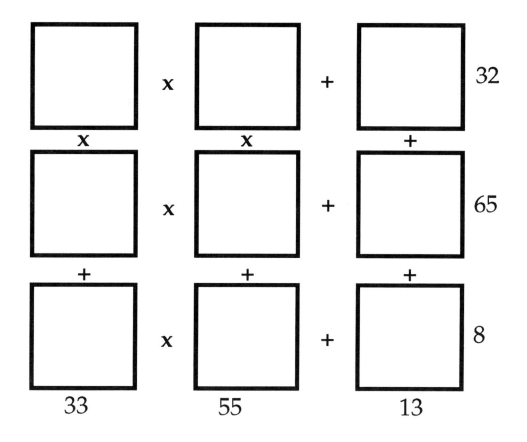

Study problem A. Then try to use the numbered tiles (1-9) to solve the other problems in a similar manner.

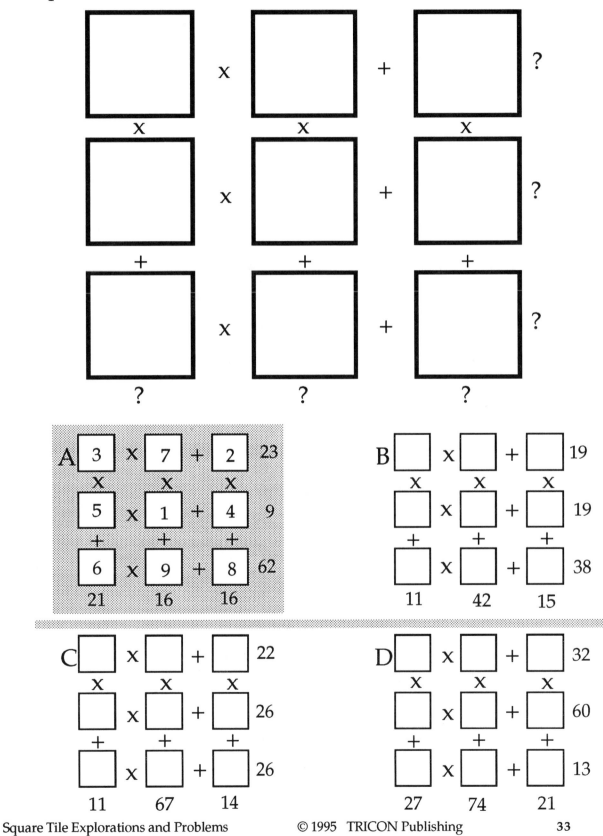

A
3	×	7	+	2	23
×		×		×	
5	×	1	+	4	9
+		+		+	
6	×	9	+	8	62
21		16		16	

B
☐	×	☐	+	☐	19
×		×		×	
☐	×	☐	+	☐	19
+		+		+	
☐	×	☐	+	☐	38
11		42		15	

C
☐	×	☐	+	☐	22
×		×		×	
☐	×	☐	+	☐	26
+		+		+	
☐	×	☐	+	☐	26
11		67		14	

D
☐	×	☐	+	☐	32
×		×		×	
☐	×	☐	+	☐	60
+		+		+	
☐	×	☐	+	☐	13
27		74		21	

Study the given example. Then try to use the nine numbered tiles (1-9) to help you determine which numbers should be placed in the boxes. Score one point for each of the six problems that you can solve in 5 minutes.

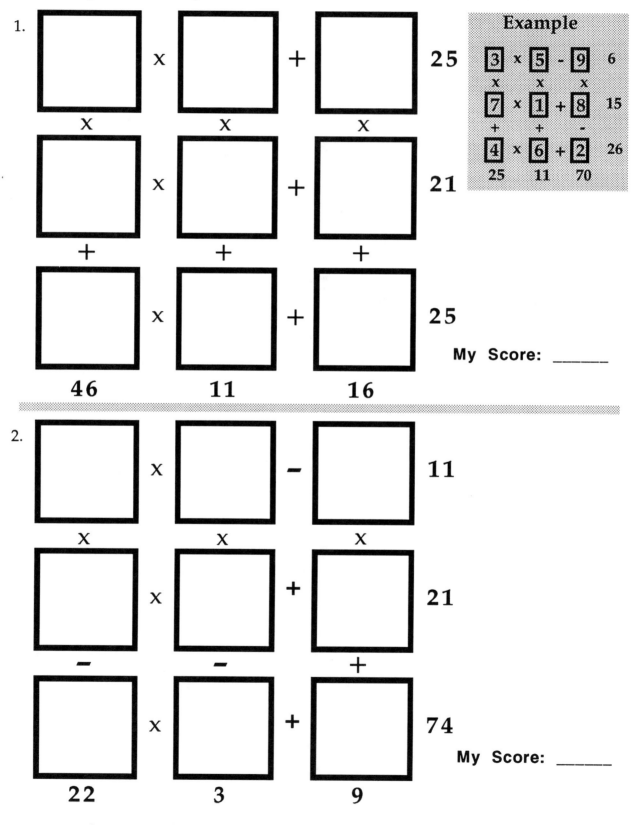

1.

☐ x ☐ + ☐   25

x   x   x

☐ x ☐ + ☐   21

+   +   +

☐ x ☐ + ☐   25

46   11   16

Example

3 x 5 - 9	6
x x x	
7 x 1 + 8	15
+ + -	
4 x 6 + 2	26
25 11 70	

My Score: _____

2.

☐ x ☐ - ☐   11

x   x   x

☐ x ☐ + ☐   21

-    -   +

☐ x ☐ + ☐   74

22   3   9

My Score: _____

Square Tile Explorations and Problems

Study the given example. Then try to use the nine numbered tiles (1-9) to help you determine which numbers should be placed in the boxes. Score one point for each of the six problems that you can solve in 5 minutes.

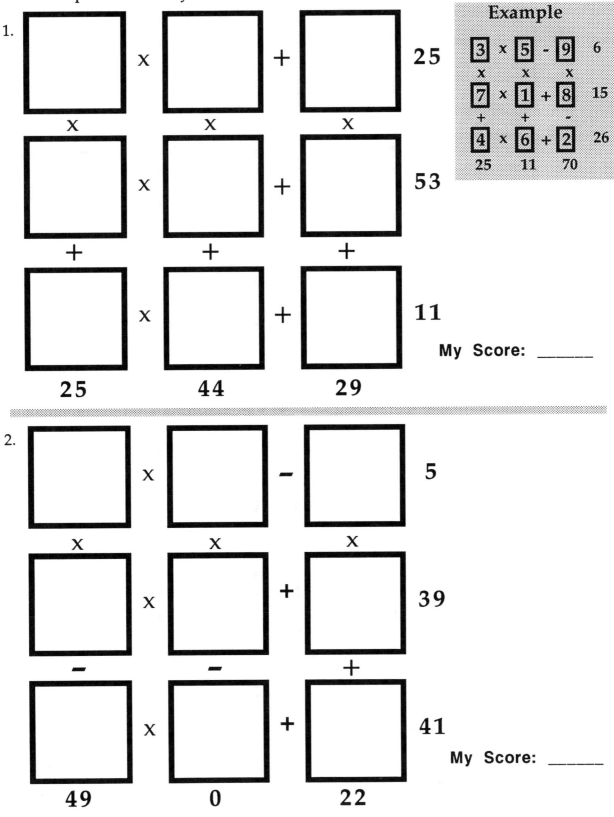

Example

3	x	5	-	9	6
x		x		x	
7	x	1	+	8	15
+		+		-	
4	x	6	+	2	26
25		11		70	

1.

	x		+		25
x		x		x	
	x		+		53
+		+		+	
	x		+		11
25		44		29	

My Score: _____

2.

	x		-		5
x		x		x	
	x		+		39
-		-		+	
	x		+		41
49		0		22	

My Score: _____

Study the given example. Then try to use the nine numbered tiles (1-9) to help you determine which numbers should be placed in the boxes. Score one point for each of the six problems that you can solve in 5 minutes.

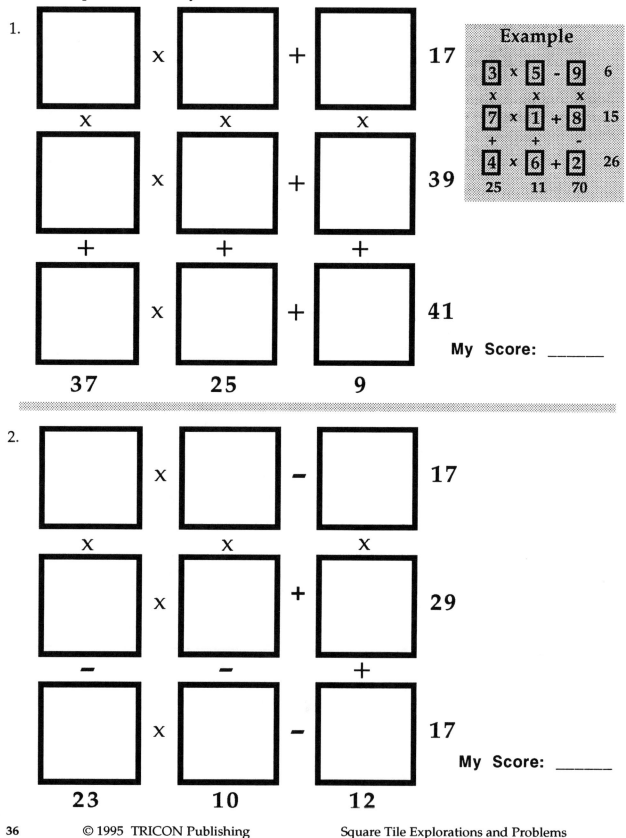

Example

☐ × ☐ − ☐ 6
3   5   9

×   ×   ×

☐ × ☐ + ☐ 15
7   1   8

+   +   −

☐ × ☐ + ☐ 26
4   6   2
25   11   70

1. ☐ × ☐ + ☐ 17

   ×   ×   ×

   ☐ × ☐ + ☐ 39

   +   +   +

   ☐ × ☐ + ☐ 41

   37   25   9

My Score: _____

2. ☐ × ☐ − ☐ 17

   ×   ×   ×

   ☐ × ☐ + ☐ 29

   −   −   +

   ☐ × ☐ − ☐ 17

   23   10   12

My Score: _____

Study the given example. Then try to use the nine numbered tiles (1-9) to help you determine which numbers should be placed in the boxes. Score one point for each of the six problems that you can solve in 5 minutes.

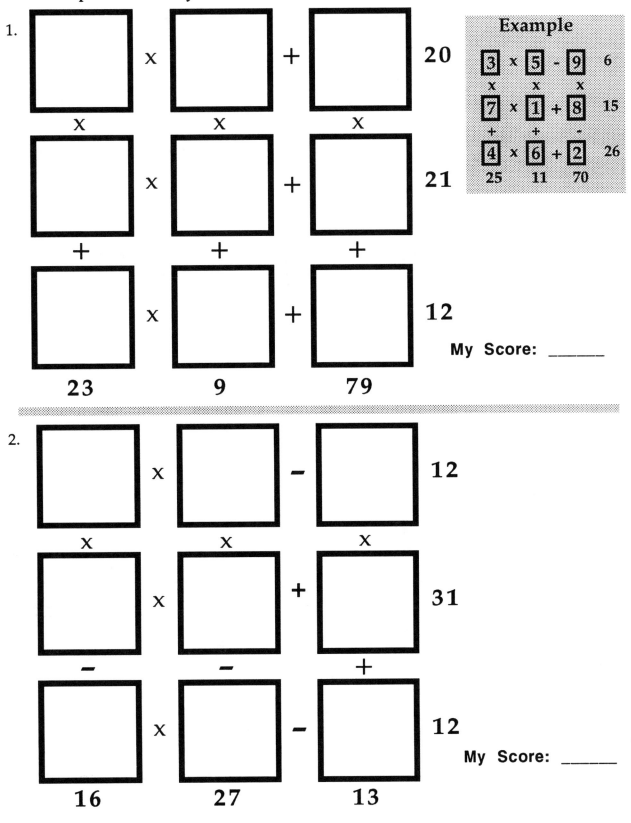

1.

☐ x ☐ + ☐   20

x   x   x

☐ x ☐ + ☐   21

+   +   +

☐ x ☐ + ☐   12

23   9   79

Example

3 x 5 - 9   6

x   x   x

7 x 1 + 8   15

+   +   -

4 x 6 + 2   26

25   11   70

My Score: _____

2.

☐ x ☐ - ☐   12

x   x   x

☐ x ☐ + ☐   31

-   -   +

☐ x ☐ - ☐   12

16   27   13

My Score: _____

Study the given example. Then randomly select four of the nine numbered tiles. Your goal is to use the selected numbers to complete the other exercises in a similar manner. Score 1 point for each correct equation.

Example: 2, 3, 4, 7

$1 = (3+7)/2 - 4$ $2 = 3+7 - 2\times4$ $3 = 3\times4 - 2 - 7$

$4 = 7 - (2+4) + 3$ $5 = (3+7) \div (4/2)$ $6 = 4 + 7 - 2 - 3$

$7 = 2\times7 - 3 - 4$ $8 = 7 - 4 + 2 + 3$ $9 = (2+7)(4-3)$

A. Digits selected: ___ ___ ___ ___   My Score: ____

$1 = \underline{\hspace{3cm}}$ $2 = \underline{\hspace{3cm}}$ $3 = \underline{\hspace{3cm}}$

$4 = \underline{\hspace{3cm}}$ $5 = \underline{\hspace{3cm}}$ $6 = \underline{\hspace{3cm}}$

$7 = \underline{\hspace{3cm}}$ $8 = \underline{\hspace{3cm}}$ $9 = \underline{\hspace{3cm}}$

B. Digits selected: ___ ___ ___ ___   My Score: ____

$1 = \underline{\hspace{3cm}}$ $2 = \underline{\hspace{3cm}}$ $3 = \underline{\hspace{3cm}}$

$4 = \underline{\hspace{3cm}}$ $5 = \underline{\hspace{3cm}}$ $6 = \underline{\hspace{3cm}}$

$7 = \underline{\hspace{3cm}}$ $8 = \underline{\hspace{3cm}}$ $9 = \underline{\hspace{3cm}}$

C. Digits selected: ___ ___ ___ ___   My Score: ____

$1 = \underline{\hspace{3cm}}$ $2 = \underline{\hspace{3cm}}$ $3 = \underline{\hspace{3cm}}$

$4 = \underline{\hspace{3cm}}$ $5 = \underline{\hspace{3cm}}$ $6 = \underline{\hspace{3cm}}$

$7 = \underline{\hspace{3cm}}$ $8 = \underline{\hspace{3cm}}$ $9 = \underline{\hspace{3cm}}$

Study the given example. Then randomly select five of the nine numbered tiles. Your goal is to use the selected numbers to complete the other exercises in a similar manner. Score 1 point for each correct equation.

Example: 1, 2, 4, 7, 9

$1 = (9+7)/4 - 1 - 2$ $2 = (7+9)/4 - 1 \times 2$ $3 = (7+9)/2 - (1+4)$

$4 = 1 \times 4 + 9 - (2+7)$ $5 = (2+7)/9 + 1 \times 4$ $6 = 9/(1+2) + 7 - 4$

$7 = 9 + 7 - 2 \times 4 - 1$ $8 = 1 \times 2 \times (9+7)/4$ $9 = 2 \times 7 + 4 - 1 \times 9$

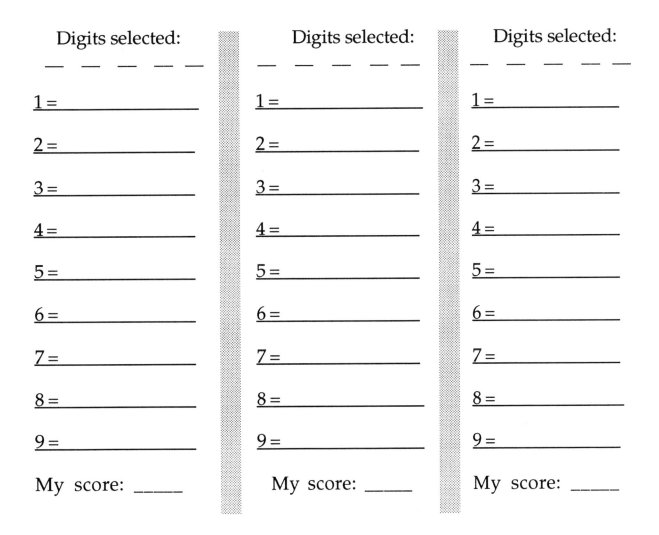

Digits selected:

— — — — —

1 = _____

2 = _____

3 = _____

4 = _____

5 = _____

6 = _____

7 = _____

8 = _____

9 = _____

My score: _____

Digits selected:

— — — — —

1 = _____

2 = _____

3 = _____

4 = _____

5 = _____

6 = _____

7 = _____

8 = _____

9 = _____

My score: _____

Digits selected:

— — — — —

1 = _____

2 = _____

3 = _____

4 = _____

5 = _____

6 = _____

7 = _____

8 = _____

9 = _____

My score: _____

Randomly place five of the nine numbered tiles on the target squares A, B, C, D, and E. Then try to use the four remaining numbered tiles to form possible expressions whose answers are the target digits. Score one point for each correct solution.

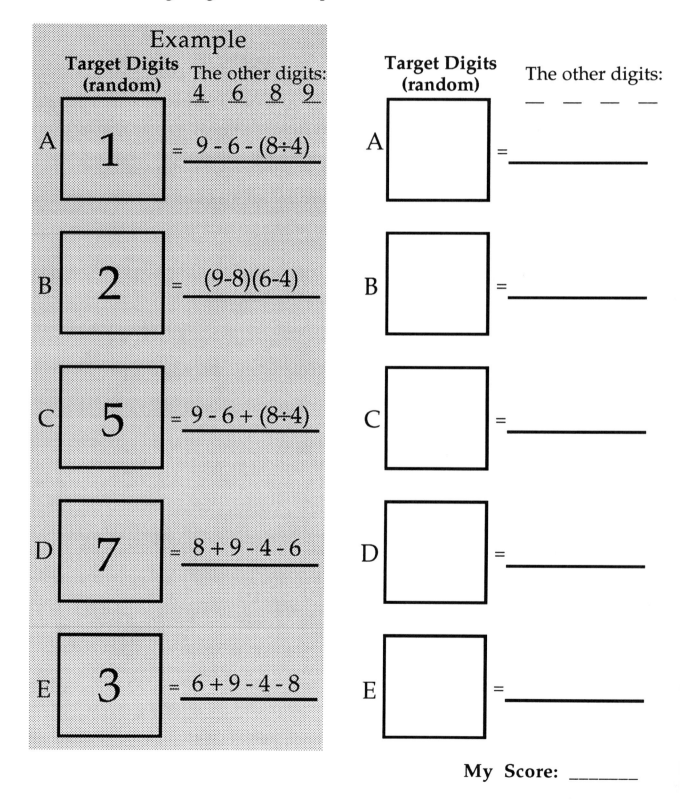

Example

Target Digits (random)   The other digits: 4 6 8 9

A   **1** $= 9 - 6 - (8 \div 4)$

B   **2** $= (9-8)(6-4)$

C   **5** $= 9 - 6 + (8 \div 4)$

D   **7** $= 8 + 9 - 4 - 6$

E   **3** $= 6 + 9 - 4 - 8$

Target Digits (random)   The other digits: __ __ __ __

A   [   ]   = _____

B   [   ]   = _____

C   [   ]   = _____

D   [   ]   = _____

E   [   ]   = _____

My Score: _____

Square Tile Explorations and Problems

Randomly place five of the nine numbered tiles on the target squares A, B, C, D, and E. Then try to use the four remaining numbered tiles to form possible expressions whose answers are the target digits. Score one point for each correct solution.

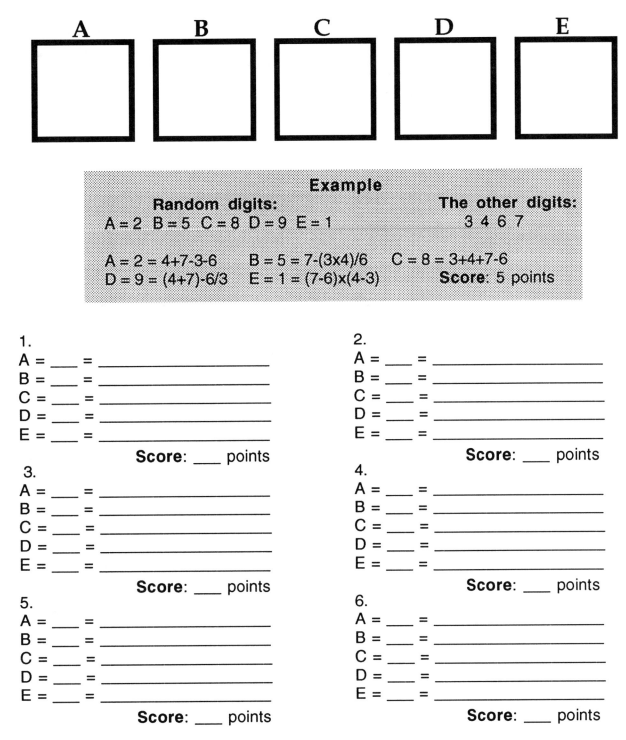

A   B   C   D   E

Example
Random digits: **The other digits:**
A = 2 B = 5 C = 8 D = 9 E = 1   3 4 6 7

A = 2 = 4+7-3-6   B = 5 = 7-(3x4)/6   C = 8 = 3+4+7-6
D = 9 = (4+7)-6/3   E = 1 = (7-6)x(4-3)   **Score**: 5 points

1.
A = ___ = _____
B = ___ = _____
C = ___ = _____
D = ___ = _____
E = ___ = _____
                Score: ___ points

2.
A = ___ = _____
B = ___ = _____
C = ___ = _____
D = ___ = _____
E = ___ = _____
                Score: ___ points

3.
A = ___ = _____
B = ___ = _____
C = ___ = _____
D = ___ = _____
E = ___ = _____
                Score: ___ points

4.
A = ___ = _____
B = ___ = _____
C = ___ = _____
D = ___ = _____
E = ___ = _____
                Score: ___ points

5.
A = ___ = _____
B = ___ = _____
C = ___ = _____
D = ___ = _____
E = ___ = _____
                Score: ___ points

6.
A = ___ = _____
B = ___ = _____
C = ___ = _____
D = ___ = _____
E = ___ = _____
                Score: ___ points

Two players take turns selecting three numeral tiles in trying to complete one of the expressions (A or B) so that its answer is one of the numbers not already covered on the playing board on the left. If the number is on the board and is not already covered, the player puts a marker on that square; otherwise, that player loses his/her turn. The first player to get 3-in-a-line in any direction wins the game.

1.

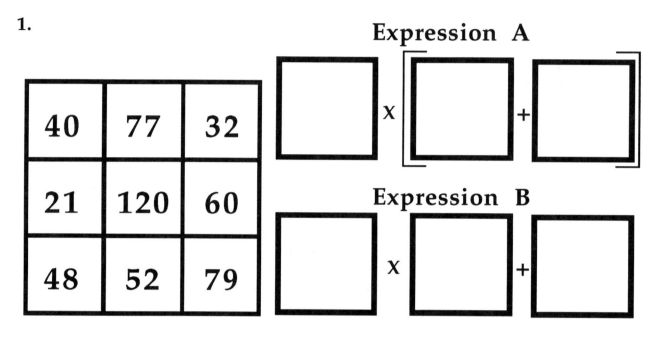

40	77	32
21	120	60
48	52	79

Expression A

☐ X ☐ + ☐

Expression B

☐ X ☐ + ☐

2.

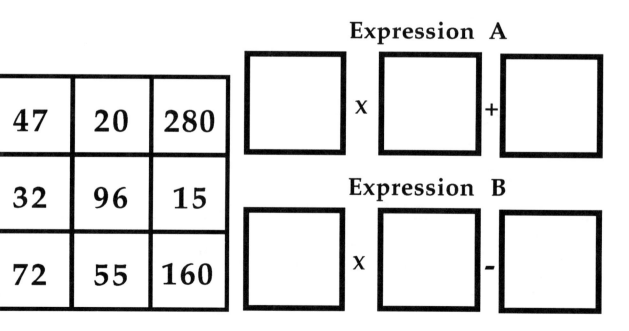

47	20	280
32	96	15
72	55	160

Expression A

☐ X ☐ + ☐

Expression B

☐ X ☐ - ☐

Square Tile Explorations and Problems

Two players take turns selecting three numeral tiles in trying to complete one of the expressions (A or B) so that its answer is one of the numbers not already covered on the playing board on the left. If the number is on the board and is not already covered, the player puts a marker on that square; otherwise, that player loses his/her turn. The first player to get 3-in-a-line in any direction wins the game.

1.

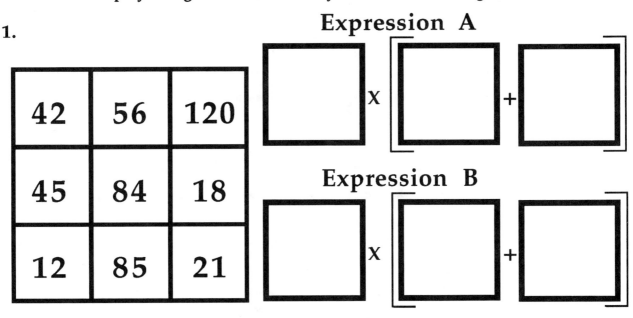

42	56	120
45	84	18
12	85	21

Expression A

☐ X ☐ + ☐

Expression B

☐ X ☐ + ☐

2.

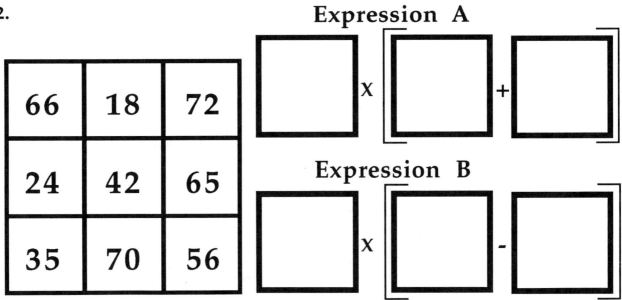

66	18	72
24	42	65
35	70	56

Expression A

☐ X ☐ + ☐

Expression B

☐ X ☐ - ☐

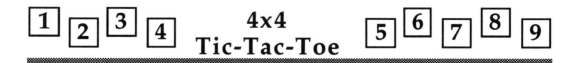

4x4
Tic-Tac-Toe

Two players take turns selecting any three of the numbered tiles (1-9) in trying to complete expression A, B, or C so that its answer is one of the numbers on the playing board that is not covered. If the number is on the board and is not already covered, the player puts a marker on that square; otherwise, that player loses his/her turn. Play continues until one player gets 3-in-a-line vertically, horizontally, or diagonally. That player wins the game.

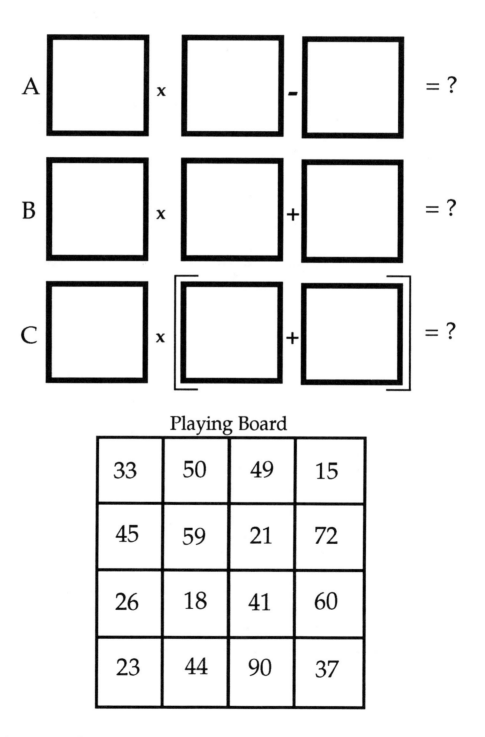

Playing Board

33	50	49	15
45	59	21	72
26	18	41	60
23	44	90	37

Square Tile Explorations and Problems

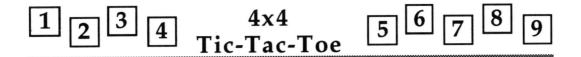
Two players take turns selecting any three of the numbered tiles (1-9) in trying to complete expression A, B, or C so that its answer is one of the numbers on the playing board that is not covered. If the number is on the board and is not already covered, the player puts a marker on that square; otherwise, that player loses his/her turn. Play continues until one player gets 3-in-a-line vertically, horizontally, or diagonally. That player wins the game.

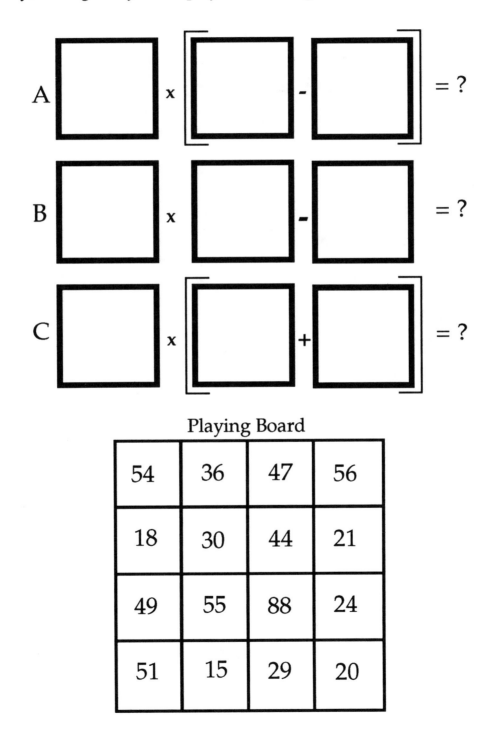

A   ☐ x [☐ - ☐] = ?

B   ☐ x ☐ - ☐ = ?

C   ☐ x [☐ + ☐] = ?

Playing Board

54	36	47	56
18	30	44	21
49	55	88	24
51	15	29	20

Use the numbered tiles (1-9) to form numbers that will satisfy the conditions stated for each of the below problems.

A	B	C	D	E	F	G

1. **AB is divisible by 2**   **ABC is divisible by 3**   **ABCD is divisible by 4**
   12/2 = 6   **123/3 = 41**   **1236/4 = 309**
   ABCDE is divisible by 5   **ABCDEFG is divisible by 6**   **A B C D E F G**
   12365/5 = 2473   **1236594/6 = 206099**   **1 2 3 6 5 9 4**

2. AB is divisible by 3   ABC is divisible by 2   ABCD is divisible by 4

   ABCDE is divisible by 6   ABCDEFG is divisible by 9   A B C D E F G

3. AB is divisible by 4   ABC is divisible by 6   ABCD is divisible by 8

   ABCDE is divisible by 2   ABCDEFG is divisible by 3   A B C D E F G

4. AB is divisible by 6   ABC is divisible by 4   ABCD is divisible by 9

   ABCDE is divisible by 4   ABCDEFG is divisible by 2   A B C D E F G

5. AB is divisible by 9   ABC is divisible by 5   ABCD is divisible by 8

   ABCDE is divisible by 3   ABCDEFG is divisible by 4   A B C D E F G

Rules:

a. Two players take turns selecting 3 of the 9 numbered tiles.

b. Place the tiles on the playing board in trying to form an expression whose unmarked answer is on the game board.

c. Mark the answer with your marker on the game board.

The first player to get 4 markers in a line (horizontally, diagonally, or vertically) is the winner.

Playing Board

$$\boxed{} \times \boxed{} - \boxed{} = ?$$

Game Board

13	52	14	21	66	50
3	21	30	36	9	37
17	57	41	2	45	69
53	15	6	51	34	60
12	37	44	29	59	27
6	39	19	50	49	44

Rules:

a. Randomly select one of the numbered tiles and place it on the Target Number square.

b. Randomly select 4 of the remaining numbered tiles. Use these tiles in trying to form an expression whose answer is 3 or less from the target number.

Scoring:	3 points if you get the target number
	2 points if the answer is 2 or less from the target number
	1 point if the answer is 3 or less from the target number
	0 points if the answer is more than 3 from the target number

Example

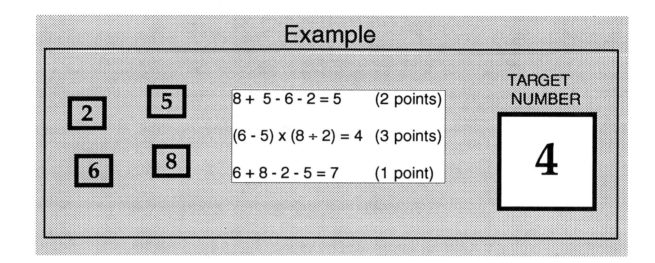

2   5

6   8

8 + 5 - 6 - 2 = 5   (2 points)

(6 - 5) x (8 ÷ 2) = 4   (3 points)

6 + 8 - 2 - 5 = 7   (1 point)

TARGET NUMBER

4

GAME BOARD

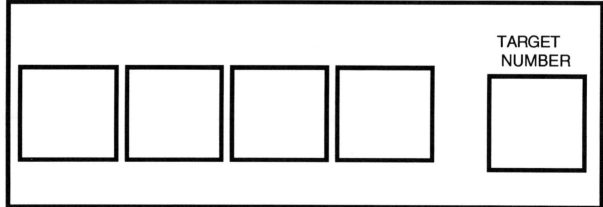

TARGET NUMBER

Randomly place three tiles to form a 3-digit target number.

TARGET NUMBER

Try to get an answer close to the target number by placing some of the remaining numbered tiles on boards A, B, C, and D. Check each answer with a calculator.

Scoring:	1 point	Guess within 100 of the target number
	3 points	Guess within 50 of the target number
	5 points	Guess within 5 of the target number

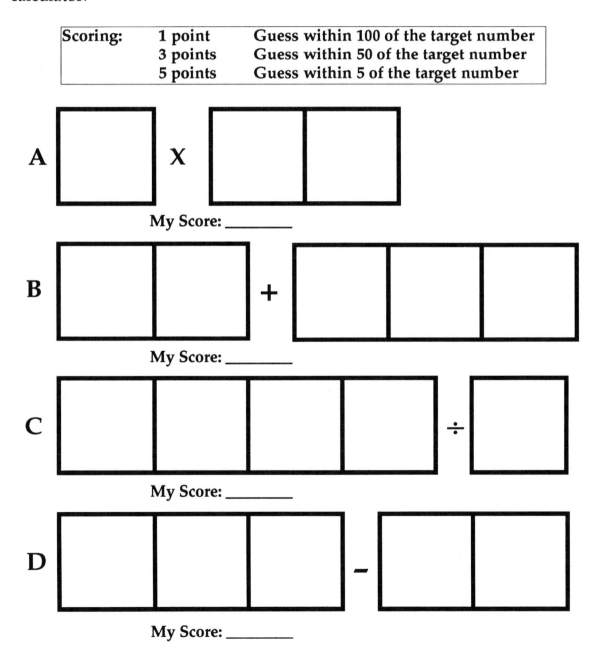

A   ☐ X ☐☐

My Score: _____

B   ☐☐ + ☐☐☐

My Score: _____

C   ☐☐☐☐ ÷ ☐

My Score: _____

D   ☐☐☐ − ☐☐

My Score: _____

Rules:

a. Randomly select 3 of the 9 numbered tiles. Place them on the playing board to form a 1-digit number (A) and a 2-digit number (BC).

b. Use the other 6 numbered tiles in trying to get two expressions whose answers are within 3 of the target numbers.

Scoring:

1 point for an expression whose answer is within 3 of the target number

3 points for an expression whose answer is the target number.

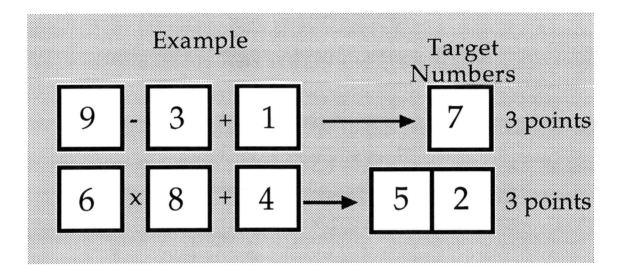

Example → Target Numbers

$9 - 3 + 1 \longrightarrow 7$ 3 points

$6 \times 8 + 4 \longrightarrow 52$ 3 points

Target Numbers

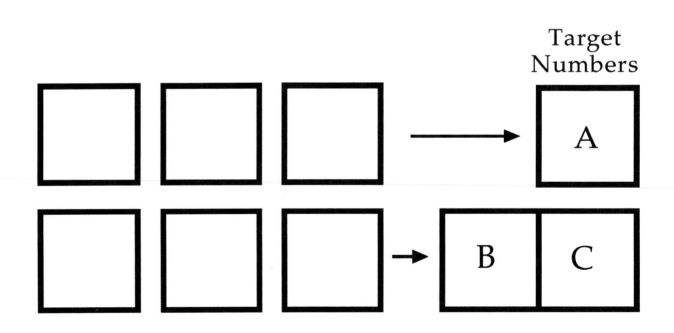

→ A

→ B C

Square Tile Explorations and Problems

Materials: Nine numbered tiles for each player.

Rules: For each of the given problems, select the five numbered tiles shown. Place the **bold** number in the Target Answer square. Then use the other four numbered tiles in trying to form expressions which have an answer equal to the target answer. Write your correct expressions next to each problem.

Scoring: 1 point for each equation whose answer is the target number.

> **Example**
> Selected numbers: **9**, 3, 4, 7, 8
>
> Equations:
>
> $$(7 + 8) \div 3 + 4 = 9 \qquad (7 - 4) + 3 + 8 = 9$$

Selected numbers	Equation		Selected numbers	Equation
1. **5**, 1, 2, 3, 7	———————		8. **2**, 3, 4, 6, 8	———————
2. **9**, 1, 2, 7, 8	———————		9. **6**, 1, 2, 5, 7	———————
3. **9**, 2, 3, 4, 6	———————		10. **6**, 1, 2, 3, 8	———————
4. **4**, 3, 6, 7, 9	———————		11. **9**, 3, 4, 7, 8	———————
5. **6**, 1, 5, 7, 8	———————		12. **7**, 2, 3, 8, 9	———————
6. **7**, 1, 3, 4, 8	———————		13. **5**, 1, 2, 3, 6	———————
7. **5**, 3, 6, 8, 9	———————		14. **6**, 2, 3, 4, 9	———————

My Score ———

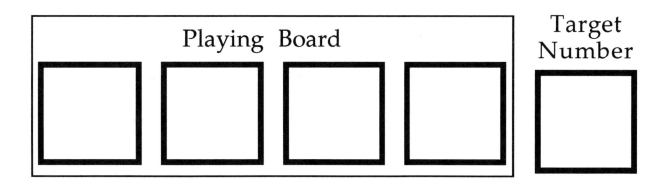

Playing Board

Target Number

Materials: Nine numbered tiles for each player.

Rules:

1. 2-4 players take turns being the leader.
2. The leader randomly selects five numbered tiles. The other players then select those same tiles from their set of tiles.
3. The leader randomly places a tile on the target number square. The other players do the same.
4. All players then use the remaining four tiles in trying to form an expression whose answer is as close as possible to the target number. Every player then writes his/her expression.
5. The player whose answer is closest to the target number scores 1 point. On ties, those players all score 1 point.
6. The first player that gets <u>six</u> points wins the game.

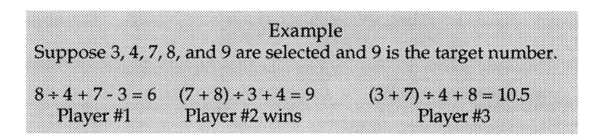

Example

Suppose 3, 4, 7, 8, and 9 are selected and 9 is the target number.

$8 \div 4 + 7 - 3 = 6$ $(7 + 8) \div 3 + 4 = 9$ $(3 + 7) \div 4 + 8 = 10.5$
    Player #1   Player #2 wins   Player #3

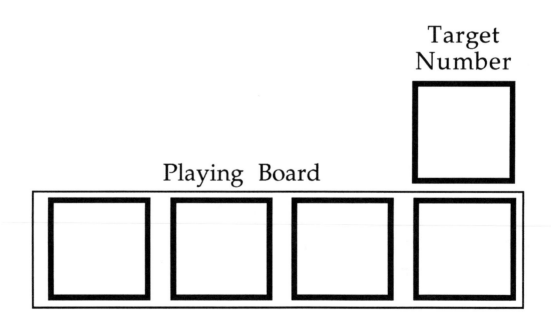

Target
Number

Playing Board

Use seven of the nine numbered tiles shown above to to find at least one solution for each of the given problems.

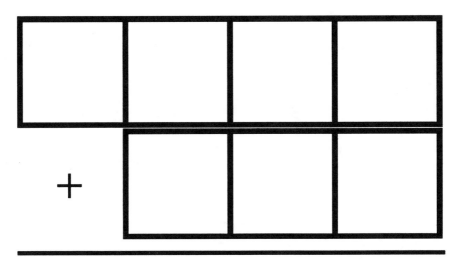

Example

a | 2 | 7 | 6 | 8 |
+ | | 3 | 4 | 5 |
‾‾‾‾‾‾‾‾‾‾‾‾‾‾
3 1 1 3

b
+
‾‾‾‾‾‾‾‾
7 1 7 2

c
+
‾‾‾‾‾‾‾‾
3 4 6 1

d
+
‾‾‾‾‾‾‾‾
4 1 9 7

e
+
‾‾‾‾‾‾‾‾
9 2 0 4

f
+
‾‾‾‾‾‾‾‾
5 0 6 1

g
+
‾‾‾‾‾‾‾‾
7 3 1 3

h
+
‾‾‾‾‾‾‾‾
3 3 5 3

i
+
‾‾‾‾‾‾‾‾
8 0 5 2

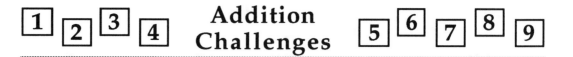
As shown in the each of the problems, place the given numbered tiles on X, Y, and Z. Then try to use five of the remaining six numbered tiles to find at least one solution for each problem.

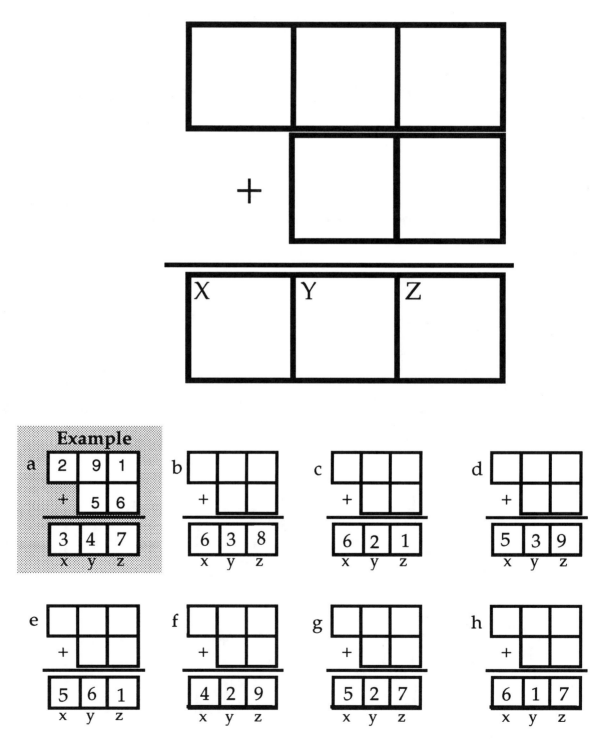

Example

a

2	9	1
+		5	6
3	4	7

x y z

b

| + | |

| 6 | 3 | 8 |

x y z

c

| + | |

| 6 | 2 | 1 |

x y z

d

| + | |

| 5 | 3 | 9 |

x y z

e

| + | |

| 5 | 6 | 1 |

x y z

f

| + | |

| 4 | 2 | 9 |

x y z

g

| + | |

| 5 | 2 | 7 |

x y z

h

| + | |

| 6 | 1 | 7 |

x y z

Square Tile Explorations and Problems

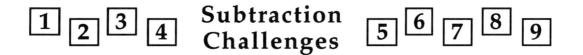
Use seven of the nine numbered tiles shown above to to find at least one solution for each of the given problems.

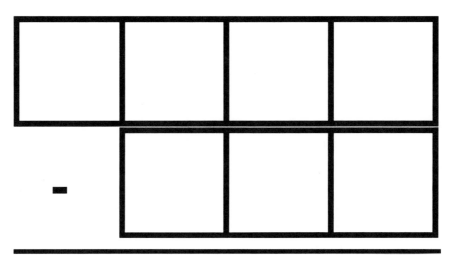

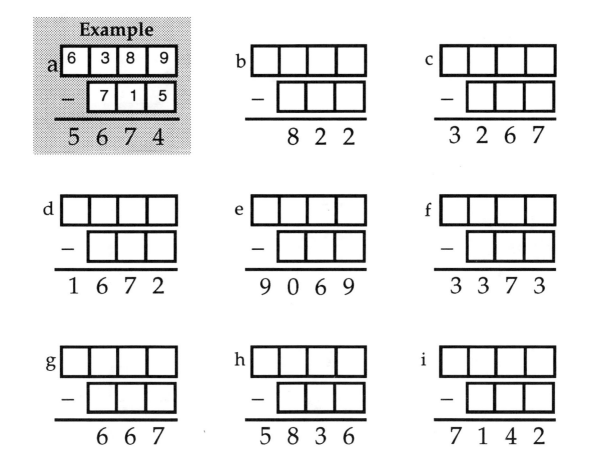

Example

a
```
  6  3  8  9
-    7  1  5
  5  6  7  4
```

b
```
-
  8  2  2
```

c
```
-
  3  2  6  7
```

d
```
-
  1  6  7  2
```

e
```
-
  9  0  6  9
```

f
```
-
  3  3  7  3
```

g
```
-
  6  6  7
```

h
```
-
  5  8  3  6
```

i
```
-
  7  1  4  2
```

As shown in each of the problems, place the given numbered tiles on X and Y. Then try to use six of the remaining seven numbered tiles to find at least one solution for each problem.

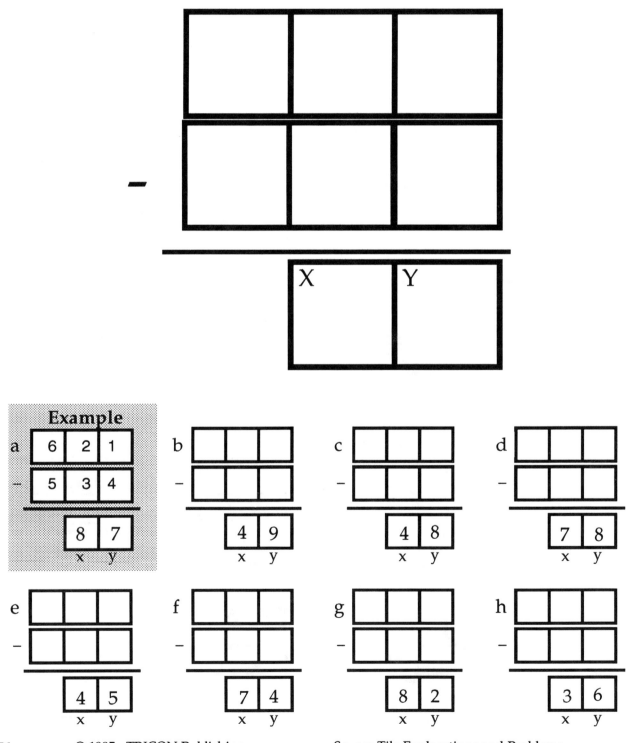

Example

a
6	2	1
5	3	4

$-$

8	7
x	y

b

4	9
x	y

c

4	8
x	y

d

7	8
x	y

e

4	5
x	y

f

7	4
x	y

g

8	2
x	y

h

3	6
x	y

Square Tile Explorations and Problems

Use the numbered tiles (1 - 9) to find at least one solution for each problem.

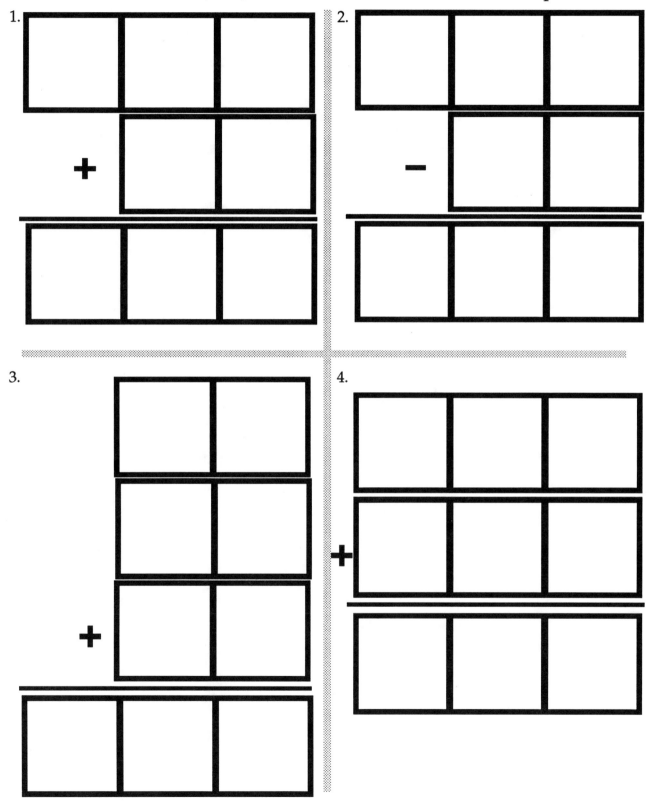

1.

2.

3.

4.

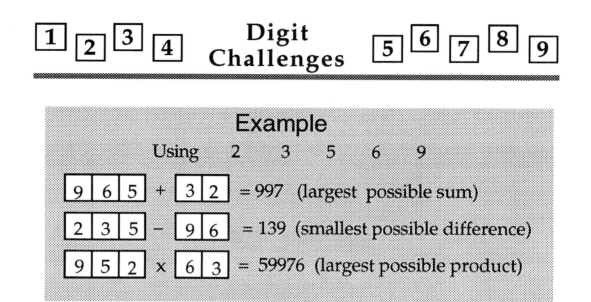

Digit Challenges

Example

Using   2   3   5   6   9

9 6 5 + 3 2 = 997 (largest possible sum)

2 3 5 – 9 6 = 139 (smallest possible difference)

9 5 2 x 6 3 = 59976 (largest possible product)

Study the above examples. Then try to use the numbered tiles (1-9) to help you find answers to the following problems.

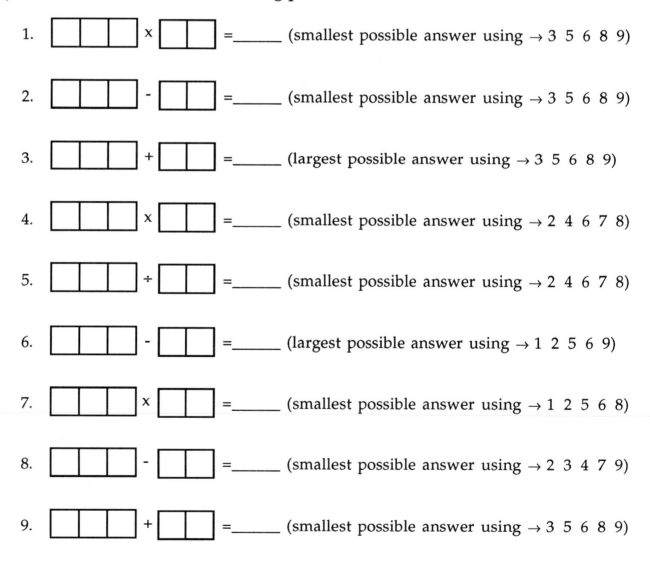

1. ☐☐☐ x ☐☐ =_____ (smallest possible answer using → 3 5 6 8 9)

2. ☐☐☐ - ☐☐ =_____ (smallest possible answer using → 3 5 6 8 9)

3. ☐☐☐ + ☐☐ =_____ (largest possible answer using → 3 5 6 8 9)

4. ☐☐☐ x ☐☐ =_____ (smallest possible answer using → 2 4 6 7 8)

5. ☐☐☐ ÷ ☐☐ =_____ (smallest possible answer using → 2 4 6 7 8)

6. ☐☐☐ - ☐☐ =_____ (largest possible answer using → 1 2 5 6 9)

7. ☐☐☐ x ☐☐ =_____ (smallest possible answer using → 1 2 5 6 8)

8. ☐☐☐ - ☐☐ =_____ (smallest possible answer using → 2 3 4 7 9)

9. ☐☐☐ + ☐☐ =_____ (smallest possible answer using → 3 5 6 8 9)

     Square Tile Explorations and Problems

Use your mental and estimation skills to help you place the numbered tiles (1-9) so that each problem is correct. Score 1 point for each correct digit.

My Score: ____

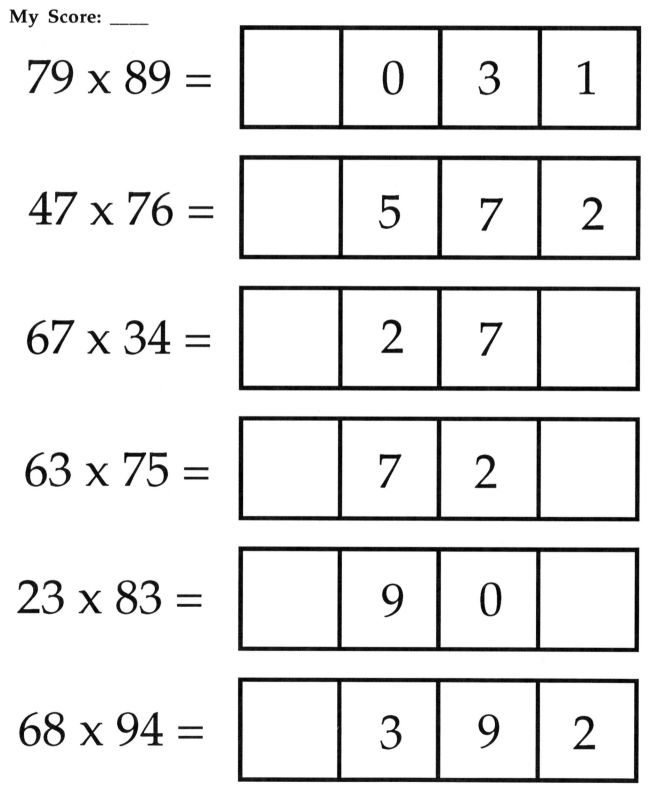

$79 \times 89 =$ | | 0 | 3 | 1 |

$47 \times 76 =$ | | 5 | 7 | 2 |

$67 \times 34 =$ | | 2 | 7 | |

$63 \times 75 =$ | | 7 | 2 | |

$23 \times 83 =$ | | 9 | 0 | |

$68 \times 94 =$ | | 3 | 9 | 2 |

Use your mental and estimation skills to help you place the numbered tiles (1-9) so that each problem is correct. After placing the tiles into the nine empty squares, check with a calculator. Score one point for each numbered tile you place correctly. My Score: _____

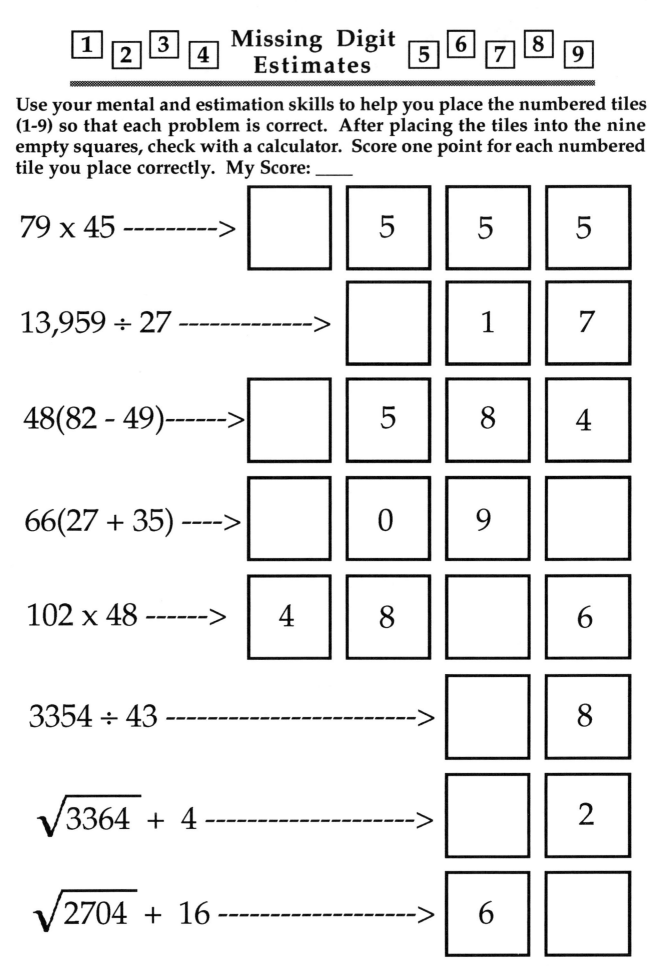

79×45 ---------> [ ] [5] [5] [5]

$13{,}959 \div 27$ -------------> [ ] [1] [7]

$48(82 - 49)$ ------> [ ] [5] [8] [4]

$66(27 + 35)$ ----> [ ] [0] [9] [ ]

102×48 ------> [4] [8] [ ] [6]

$3354 \div 43$ -----------------------------> [ ] [8]

$\sqrt{3364} + 4$ ---------------------> [ ] [2]

$\sqrt{2704} + 16$ -------------------> [6] [ ]

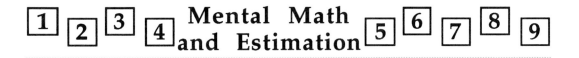

Use your mental math and estimation skills in trying to find a solution for each of the below problems. After placing six of the nine numbered tiles, check with a calculator.

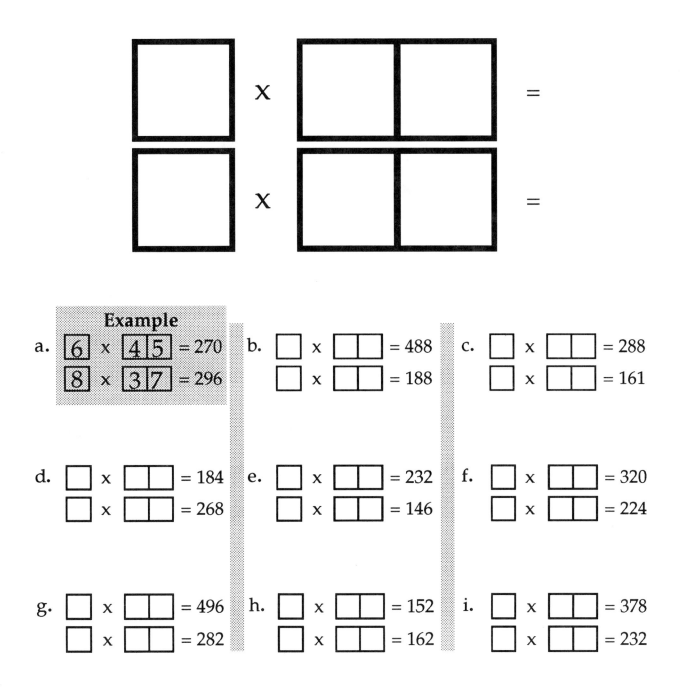

Example

a. $\boxed{6} \times \boxed{4\ 5} = 270$
$\boxed{8} \times \boxed{3\ 7} = 296$

b. $\square \times \boxed{\ \ } = 488$
$\square \times \boxed{\ \ } = 188$

c. $\square \times \boxed{\ \ } = 288$
$\square \times \boxed{\ \ } = 161$

d. $\square \times \boxed{\ \ } = 184$
$\square \times \boxed{\ \ } = 268$

e. $\square \times \boxed{\ \ } = 232$
$\square \times \boxed{\ \ } = 146$

f. $\square \times \boxed{\ \ } = 320$
$\square \times \boxed{\ \ } = 224$

g. $\square \times \boxed{\ \ } = 496$
$\square \times \boxed{\ \ } = 282$

h. $\square \times \boxed{\ \ } = 152$
$\square \times \boxed{\ \ } = 162$

i. $\square \times \boxed{\ \ } = 378$
$\square \times \boxed{\ \ } = 232$

Use your mental math and estimation skills in trying to find a solution for each of the below problems. After placing all nine numbered tiles, check with a calculator. Score 1 point for each correct answer.

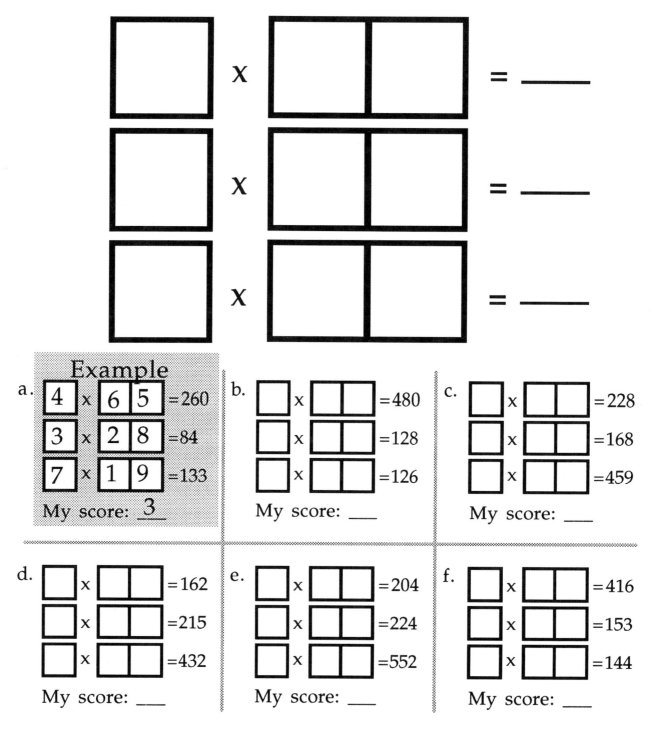

Example

a.
4	x	6	5	= 260
3	x	2	8	= 84
7	x	1	9	= 133

My score: 3

b.
☐ x ☐☐ = 480
☐ x ☐☐ = 128
☐ x ☐☐ = 126

My score: ___

c.
☐ x ☐☐ = 228
☐ x ☐☐ = 168
☐ x ☐☐ = 459

My score: ___

d.
☐ x ☐☐ = 162
☐ x ☐☐ = 215
☐ x ☐☐ = 432

My score: ___

e.
☐ x ☐☐ = 204
☐ x ☐☐ = 224
☐ x ☐☐ = 552

My score: ___

f.
☐ x ☐☐ = 416
☐ x ☐☐ = 153
☐ x ☐☐ = 144

My score: ___

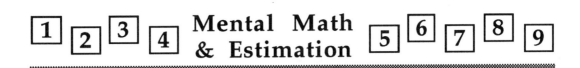

Use your mental math and estimation skills in trying to find a solution for each of the below problems. After placing all nine numbered tiles, check with a calculator. Score 1 point for each correct answer.

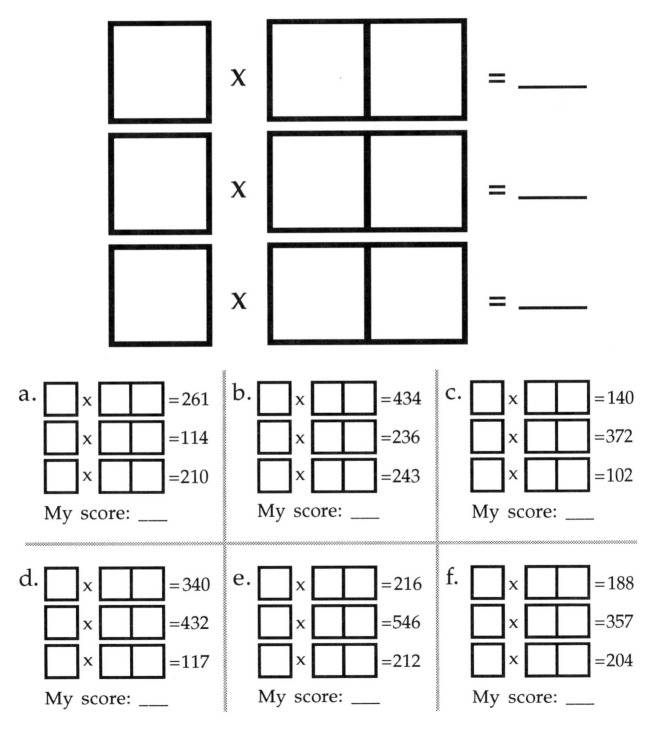

a. ☐ x ☐☐ =261
   ☐ x ☐☐ =114
   ☐ x ☐☐ =210

   My score: ___

b. ☐ x ☐☐ =434
   ☐ x ☐☐ =236
   ☐ x ☐☐ =243

   My score: ___

c. ☐ x ☐☐ =140
   ☐ x ☐☐ =372
   ☐ x ☐☐ =102

   My score: ___

d. ☐ x ☐☐ =340
   ☐ x ☐☐ =432
   ☐ x ☐☐ =117

   My score: ___

e. ☐ x ☐☐ =216
   ☐ x ☐☐ =546
   ☐ x ☐☐ =212

   My score: ___

f. ☐ x ☐☐ =188
   ☐ x ☐☐ =357
   ☐ x ☐☐ =204

   My score: ___

Use your mental and estimation skills to complete each multiplication table. Check with a calculator after placing six of the remaining seven numbered tiles.

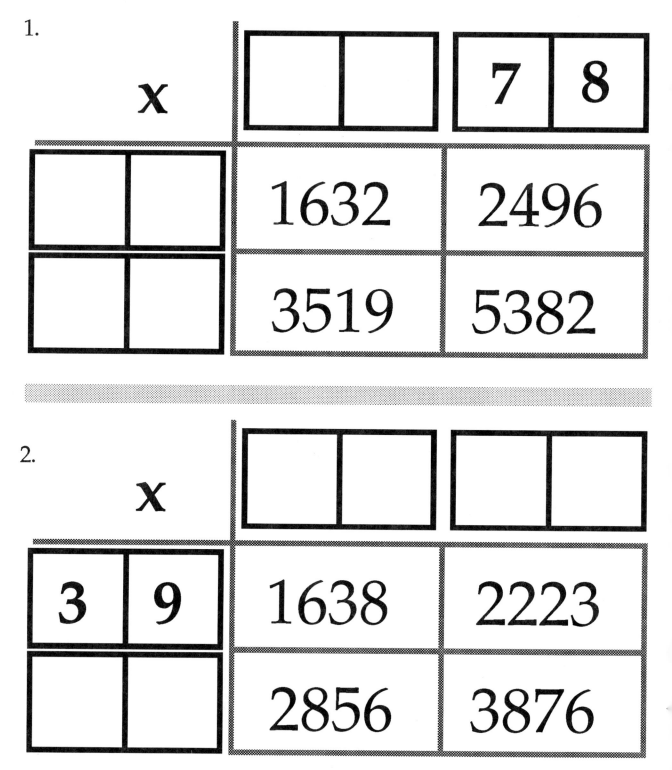

1.

x			7	8
		1632		2496
		3519		5382

2.

x				
3	9	1638		2223
		2856		3876

Use your mental and estimation skills to complete each multiplication table. Check with a calculator after placing six of the remaining seven numbered tiles.

1.

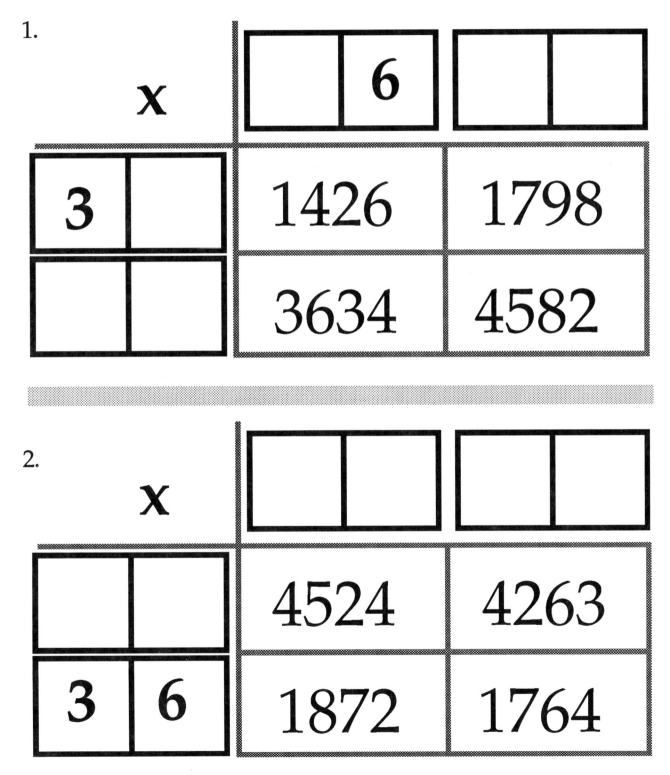

	X		**6**		
3		1426		1798	
		3634		4582	

2.

	X				
		4524		4263	
3	**6**	1872		1764	

Estimation Game

1 2 3 4 **Estimation Game** 5 6 7 8 9

Rules:

a. 2-4 players take turns randomly selecting and placing numbered tiles in each square of boards A, B, or C.

b. All players then try to guess the first and last digits in the answer.

Example: 93 x 35 = 3395; first digit = 3 last digit = 5

c. Check with a calculator after all players have written their answers.

Scoring: Both digits correct earn 1 point.

The first player that scores 5 points wins the game.

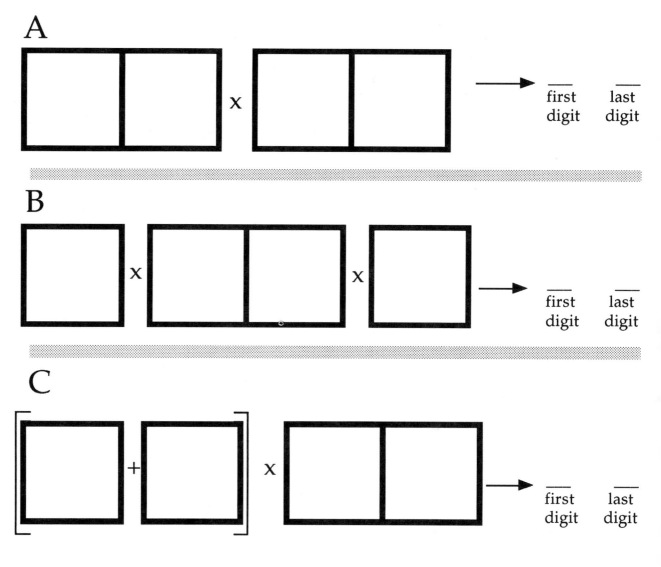

A

□□ X □□ ⟶ first digit last digit

B

□ X □□ X □ ⟶ first digit last digit

C

[□ + □] X □□ ⟶ first digit last digit

© 1995 TRICON Publishing   Square Tile Explorations and Problems

Estimation Skills

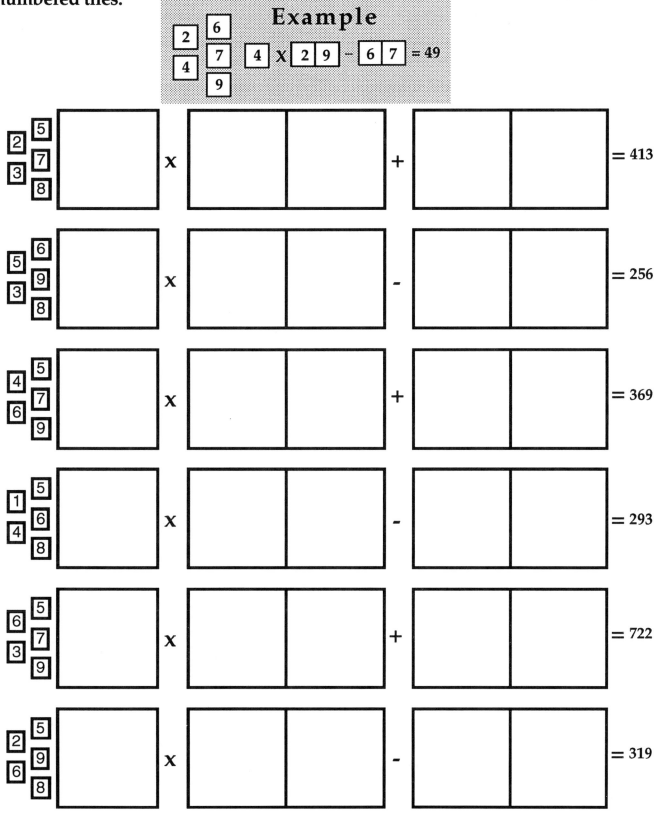

Use your mental and estimation skills in trying to correctly place the given numbered tiles.

Example

$$\boxed{4} \times \boxed{2}\,\boxed{9} - \boxed{6}\,\boxed{7} = 49$$

with tiles $\boxed{2}$, $\boxed{6}$, $\boxed{7}$, $\boxed{4}$, $\boxed{9}$

Tiles: $\boxed{2}\,\boxed{5}\,\boxed{3}\,\boxed{7}\,\boxed{8}$

$$\square \times \square\square + \square\square = 413$$

Tiles: $\boxed{5}\,\boxed{6}\,\boxed{3}\,\boxed{9}\,\boxed{8}$

$$\square \times \square\square - \square\square = 256$$

Tiles: $\boxed{4}\,\boxed{5}\,\boxed{6}\,\boxed{7}\,\boxed{9}$

$$\square \times \square\square + \square\square = 369$$

Tiles: $\boxed{1}\,\boxed{5}\,\boxed{4}\,\boxed{6}\,\boxed{8}$

$$\square \times \square\square - \square\square = 293$$

Tiles: $\boxed{6}\,\boxed{5}\,\boxed{3}\,\boxed{7}\,\boxed{9}$

$$\square \times \square\square + \square\square = 722$$

Tiles: $\boxed{2}\,\boxed{5}\,\boxed{6}\,\boxed{9}\,\boxed{8}$

$$\square \times \square\square - \square\square = 319$$

Rules:

a. 2-4 players take turns placing the nine numbered tiles.

b. All players then write estimates for the square roots.

c. Check with a calculator.

Scoring: 1 point for the estimate closest to the exact answer. On ties, those players all score 1 point.

The first player that scores 9 points wins the game.

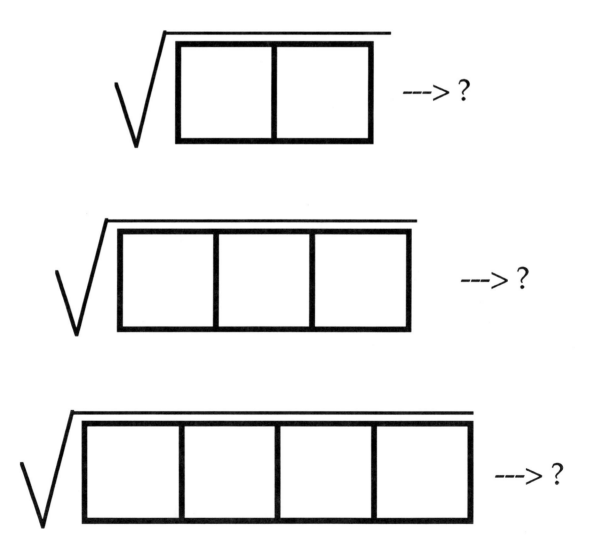

2-4 players take turns randomly placing the numbered tiles (1-9) into the empty squares. All players then estimate an answer for each problem.
Check with a calculator. The player closest to the exact answer in each case scores one point. All players with identical estimates score a point. The first player that scores seven points is the winner.

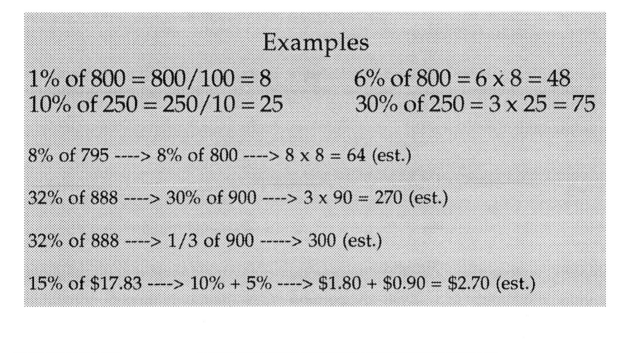

Examples

$1\% \text{ of } 800 = 800/100 = 8$ $6\% \text{ of } 800 = 6 \times 8 = 48$
$10\% \text{ of } 250 = 250/10 = 25$ $30\% \text{ of } 250 = 3 \times 25 = 75$

$8\% \text{ of } 795 \text{ ----> } 8\% \text{ of } 800 \text{ ----> } 8 \times 8 = 64 \text{ (est.)}$

$32\% \text{ of } 888 \text{ ----> } 30\% \text{ of } 900 \text{ ---> } 3 \times 90 = 270 \text{ (est.)}$

$32\% \text{ of } 888 \text{ ----> } 1/3 \text{ of } 900 \text{ -----> } 300 \text{ (est.)}$

$15\% \text{ of } \$17.83 \text{ ----> } 10\% + 5\% \text{ ----> } \$1.80 + \$0.90 = \$2.70 \text{ (est.)}$

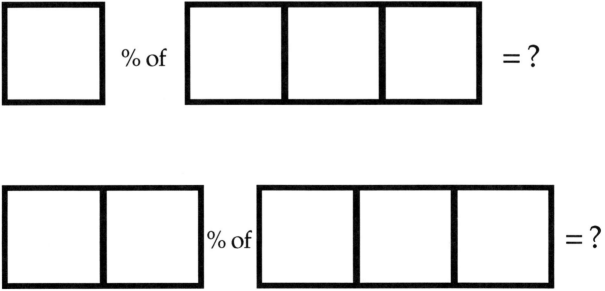

1 2 3 4 Probability Challenges 5 6 7 8 9

If each region of the spinner shown below must contain exactly one of the numbered tiles (1-9), show how 4 of the 9 tiles can be placed so that when spinning the spinner, the probability of getting:

		Possible Answers A	B	C	D
1.	an even number is 1/2	1	3	5	2
2.	an odd number is 1/4	___	___	___	___
3.	a multiple of 3 is 1/2	___	___	___	___
4.	a prime number is 1/4	___	___	___	___
5.	a perfect square is 1/8	___	___	___	___
6.	an even number is 3/4	___	___	___	___
7.	a factor of 16 is 1/2	___	___	___	___
8.	an odd prime is 3/4	___	___	___	___
9.	a factor of 110 is 7/8	___	___	___	___
10.	a perfect cube is 1/4	___	___	___	___

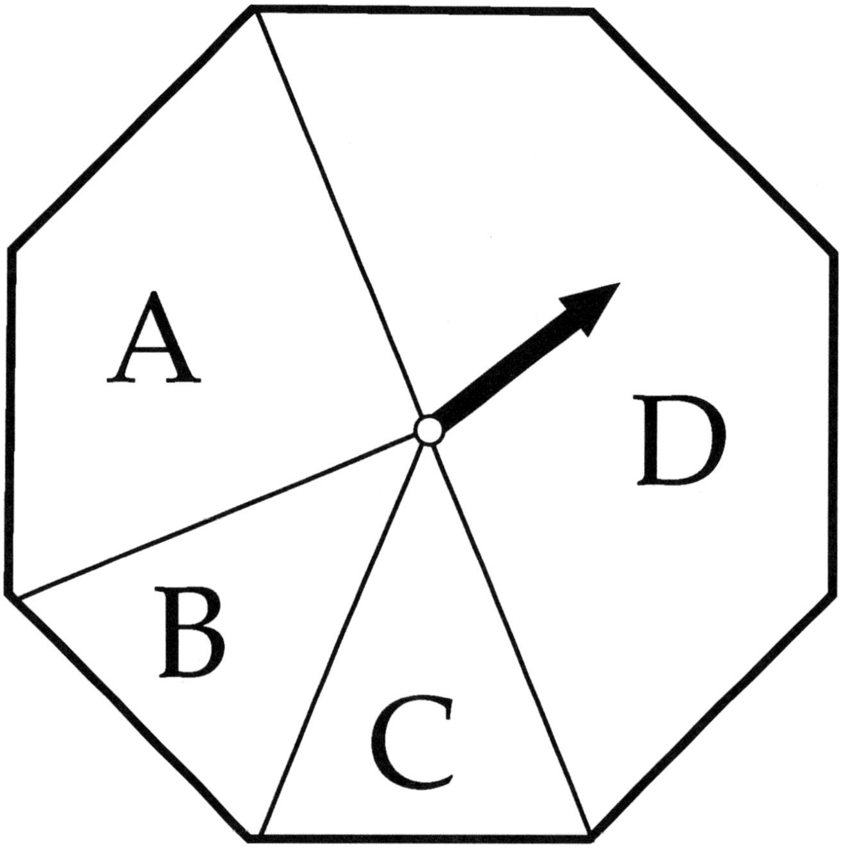

Given that two of the corner squares are prime, use the below clues to help you place six of the nine numbered tiles (1-9) on the squares A, B, C, D, E, and F.

Clues:
* All are different digits.
* The sum of all the numbers is 25.
* A is one-fourth of F
* C is twice D.
* The sum of A, B, and C is 9.
* D is not even.
* E is not a perfect square.

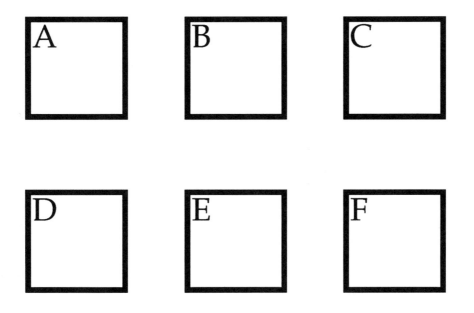

The numbered tiles (1-9) can be placed into the empty squares so that they are the answer to the given problems. For example, in number 1, the tens digit of the largest 5-digit perfect square is 5. Try to place the other tiles so that all represent a correct answer.

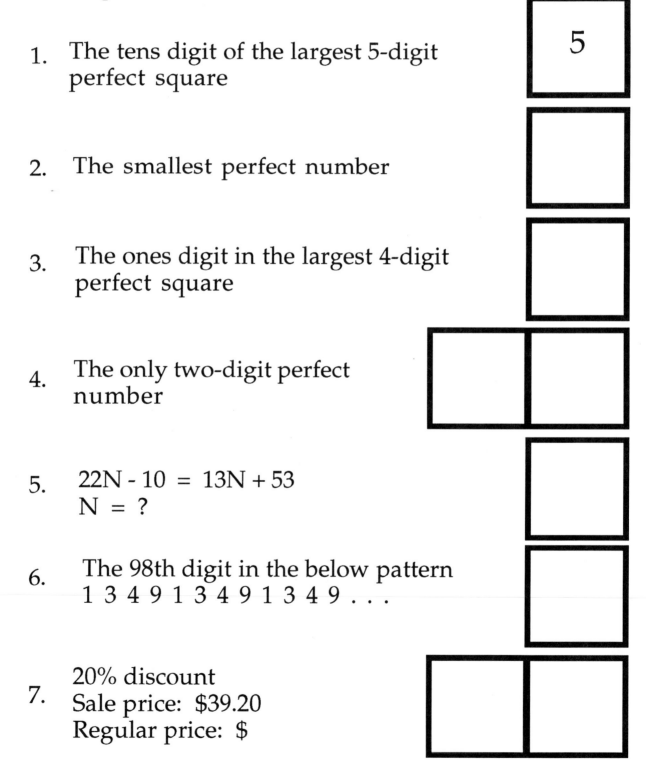

1. The tens digit of the largest 5-digit perfect square

2. The smallest perfect number

3. The ones digit in the largest 4-digit perfect square

4. The only two-digit perfect number

5. $22N - 10 = 13N + 53$
   $N = ?$

6. The 98th digit in the below pattern
   1 3 4 9 1 3 4 9 1 3 4 9 . . .

7. 20% discount
   Sale price: $39.20
   Regular price: $

Materials: Nine numbered tiles (1-9) as shown above.

1. Place 5 tiles into two sets so that each set has a sum which is a prime number.

2. Place 8 tiles into three sets so that each set has a sum which is even.

3. Place 4 tiles into two sets so that the sum in each set is a perfect square.

4. Place all 9 tiles into three sets so that the sum in each set is the same.

5. Find 3 tiles whose sum is six less than a prime number.

6. Find 3 tiles whose product is a 2-digit perfect square.

7. Find 3 tiles where the product is between 50 and 55.

8. Place 5 tiles into two sets so that the sum in each set is a perfect square.

9. Find 4 tiles where the product of their numbers is 3 times their sum.

10. Find 2 tiles where the product is 17 more than the sum.

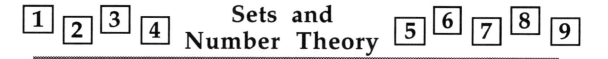
Find the number tiles in sets A and B that will satisfy the given clues for each problem.

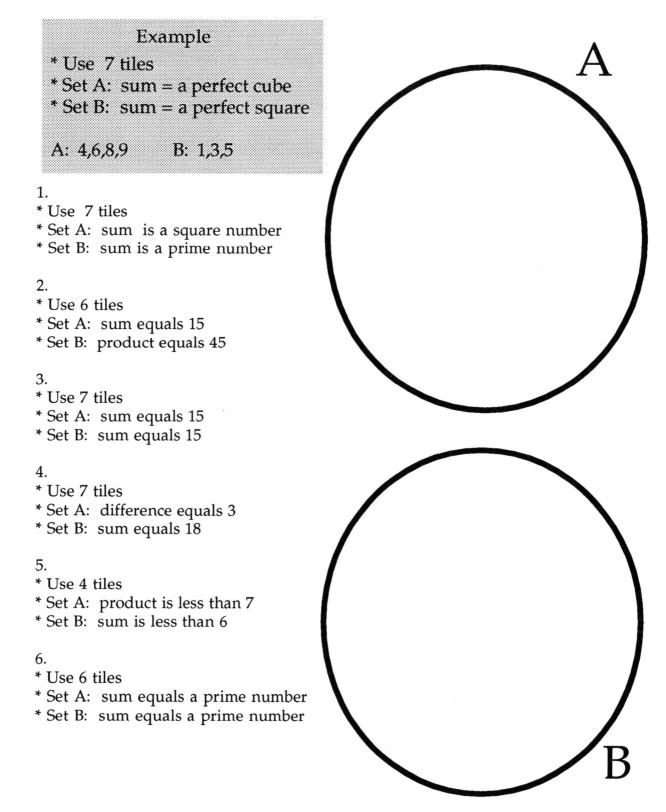

Example
* Use 7 tiles
* Set A: sum = a perfect cube
* Set B: sum = a perfect square

A: 4,6,8,9   B: 1,3,5

1.
* Use 7 tiles
* Set A: sum is a square number
* Set B: sum is a prime number

2.
* Use 6 tiles
* Set A: sum equals 15
* Set B: product equals 45

3.
* Use 7 tiles
* Set A: sum equals 15
* Set B: sum equals 15

4.
* Use 7 tiles
* Set A: difference equals 3
* Set B: sum equals 18

5.
* Use 4 tiles
* Set A: product is less than 7
* Set B: sum is less than 6

6.
* Use 6 tiles
* Set A: sum equals a prime number
* Set B: sum equals a prime number

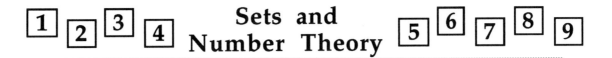

Find the number tiles in sets A , B, and C that will satisfy the given clues for each problem.

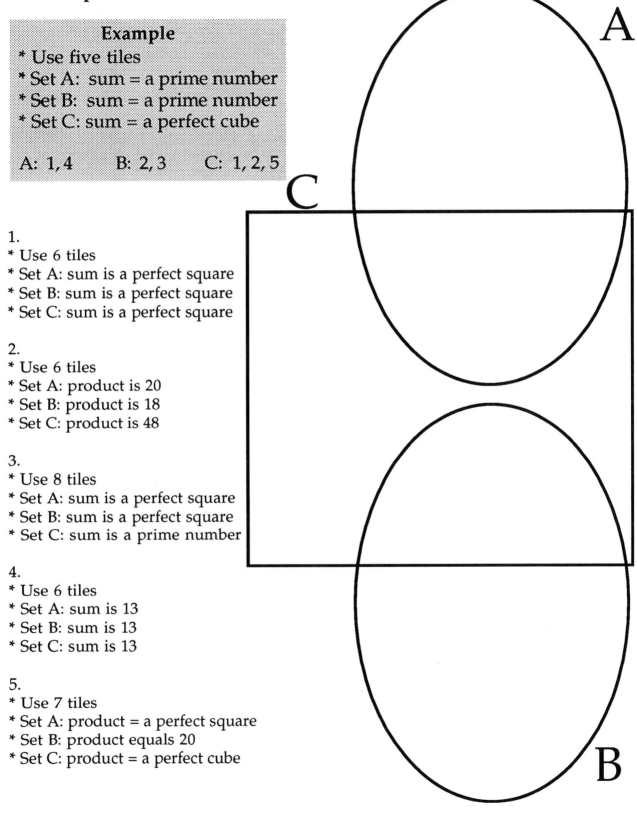

Example
* Use five tiles
* Set A: sum = a prime number
* Set B: sum = a prime number
* Set C: sum = a perfect cube

A: 1, 4   B: 2, 3   C: 1, 2, 5

1.
* Use 6 tiles
* Set A: sum is a perfect square
* Set B: sum is a perfect square
* Set C: sum is a perfect square

2.
* Use 6 tiles
* Set A: product is 20
* Set B: product is 18
* Set C: product is 48

3.
* Use 8 tiles
* Set A: sum is a perfect square
* Set B: sum is a perfect square
* Set C: sum is a prime number

4.
* Use 6 tiles
* Set A: sum is 13
* Set B: sum is 13
* Set C: sum is 13

5.
* Use 7 tiles
* Set A: product = a perfect square
* Set B: product equals 20
* Set C: product = a perfect cube

Find the number tiles in sets A and B that will satisfy the given clues for each problem.

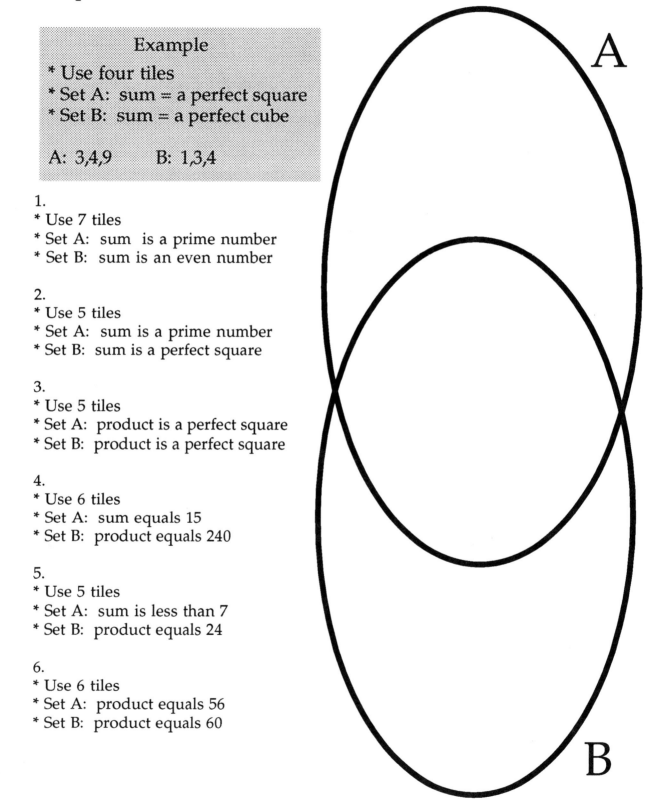

Example
* Use four tiles
* Set A: sum = a perfect square
* Set B: sum = a perfect cube

A: 3,4,9   B: 1,3,4

1.
* Use 7 tiles
* Set A: sum is a prime number
* Set B: sum is an even number

2.
* Use 5 tiles
* Set A: sum is a prime number
* Set B: sum is a perfect square

3.
* Use 5 tiles
* Set A: product is a perfect square
* Set B: product is a perfect square

4.
* Use 6 tiles
* Set A: sum equals 15
* Set B: product equals 240

5.
* Use 5 tiles
* Set A: sum is less than 7
* Set B: product equals 24

6.
* Use 6 tiles
* Set A: product equals 56
* Set B: product equals 60

Make up problems similar to the given example to be solved by your classmates.

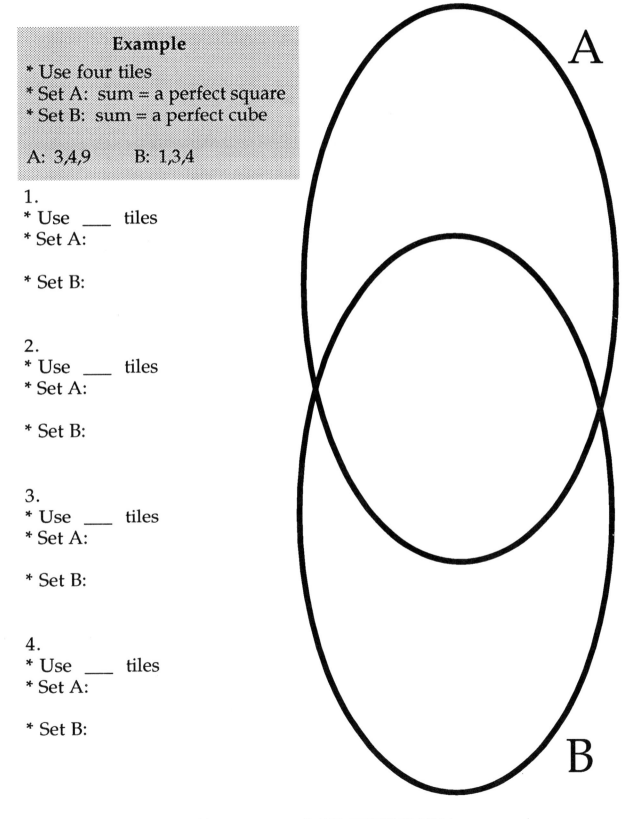

> **Example**
> * Use four tiles
> * Set A: sum = a perfect square
> * Set B: sum = a perfect cube
>
> A: 3,4,9   B: 1,3,4

1.
* Use ___ tiles
* Set A:

* Set B:

2.
* Use ___ tiles
* Set A:

* Set B:

3.
* Use ___ tiles
* Set A:

* Set B:

4.
* Use ___ tiles
* Set A:

* Set B:

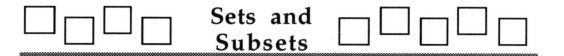

Sets and Subsets

There are exactly four different sets that can be formed by using one red tile and one blue tile.

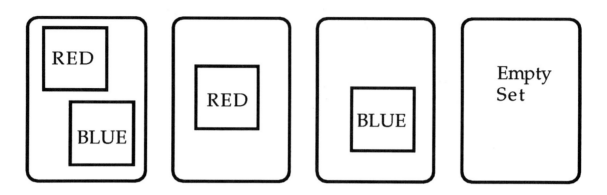

1. How many different subsets can be formed by using:
   a. one red, one blue, and one yellow tile? (Show each subset.)

   b. one red, one yellow, one blue, and one green tile?

2. How many subsets?

   {a} __2__   {a,b} __4__   {a,b,c} ____   {a,b,c,d} ____

   {a,b,c,d,e} ____   . . .   {a,b,c,d,...,k} _____

3. A set that contains N elements has _____ subsets.

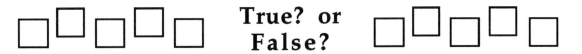

True? or False?

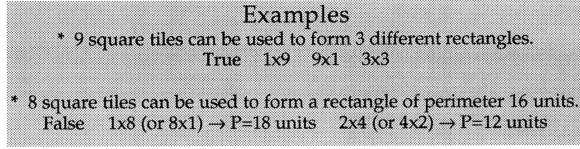

Study the below examples. Then try to complete the other problems in a similar manner.

Examples
* 9 square tiles can be used to form 3 different rectangles.
  True   1x9   9x1   3x3

* 8 square tiles can be used to form a rectangle of perimeter 16 units.
  False   1x8 (or 8x1) → P=18 units   2x4 (or 4x2) → P=12 units

1. 12 square tiles can be used to form six different rectangles.

2. 12 or less tiles can be used to form a rectangle whose area is X square units and whose perimeter is 2X units.

3. The square tiles can be used to form a rectangle of perimeter 21 units.

4. There are 6 different ways to place 24 tiles into two or more sets so that each set contains the same number of tiles.

5. The square tiles **cannot** be used to form a rectangle whose area is X square units and whose perimeter is X units.

6. 17 square tiles can be used to form a rectangle whose perimeter is a perfect square.

7. There are 27 different ways to place 33 square tiles into two disjoint sets given that each set must end up with at least 3 tiles.

8. There are 15 different ways to place seven tiles into 3 disjoint sets given that each set must end up with at least one tile.

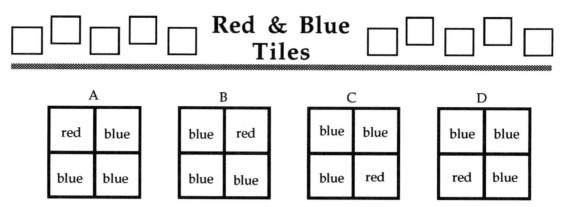

A		B		C		D	
red	blue	blue	red	blue	blue	blue	blue
blue	blue	blue	blue	blue	red	red	blue

The above figures show how one red and 3 blue square tiles can form a 2x2 square. Suppose we count these as only one "different" way since A can be rotated (turned) to form B, C, and D.

* How many "different" ways can one red and 8 blue tiles be arranged in this 3 by 3 square?

*How many "different" ways can two red and 7 blue tiles be arranged in this 3 by 3 square?

For Experts only!
How many "different" ways can three red and six blue tiles be arranged in this 3 by 3 square?

*How many "different" ways can one red and 15 blue square tiles be arranged in this 4 by 4 square?

                Square Tile Explorations and Problems

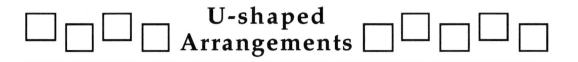

Suppose each of the below figures represents an arrangement of square tables that seat one person on each side. For example, arrangement #1 has 10 tables that can seat 22 people. Verify.

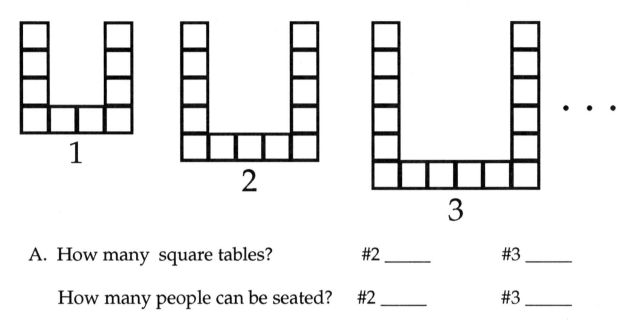

A. How many square tables?   #2 _____   #3 _____

    How many people can be seated?   #2 _____   #3 _____

B. If the pattern of U-shaped tables continues in this way, how many square tables would there be in arrangement:

#4? _____   #5? _____   #20? _____   N? _____

C. If the pattern of U-shaped tables continues in this way, how many people could be seated in arrangement:

#4? _____   #5? _____   #20? _____   N? _____

Counting Border Squares

The below figure shows that 14 square tiles are needed to surround a 2 by 3 rectangular arrangement of tiles. Also, the perimeter of the surrounded rectangle is 18 units. Verify.

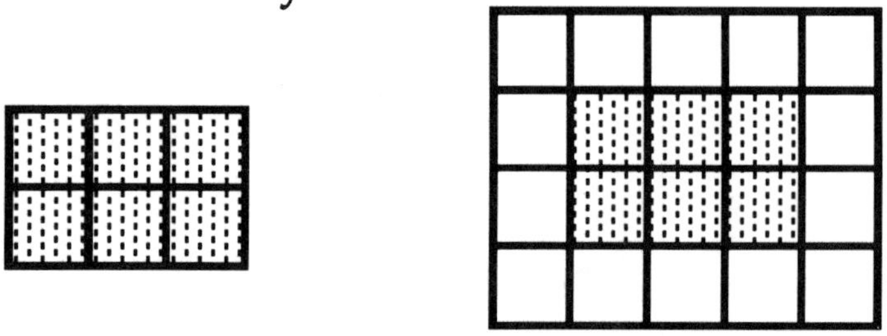

Complete the following by finding the number of square tiles that will be needed to surround the given rectangles and then find the perimeter of each surrounded rectangle.

Rectangle	# Tiles to surround	Perimeter (surrounded)
2 x 3	14	18 units
2 x 2	______	______
3 x 3	______	______
4 x 4	______	______
10 x 10	______	______
N x N	______	______
2 x 5	______	______
3 x 6	______	______
4 x 7	______	______
10 x 20	______	______
M x N	______	______

Counting
Border Squares

A. Verify each of following.

1. A 3 by 3 square grid has 8 border squares.

2. A 5 by 5 square grid has 16 border squares.

3. A 4 by 7 square grid has 18 border squares.

4. A 5 by 9 square grid has 24 border squares.

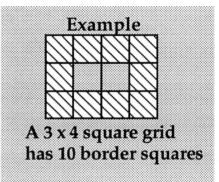

Example

A 3 x 4 square grid
has 10 border squares

B. Find the missing parts.

1. A 6 by 6 square grid has _____ border squares.

2. A 10 by 10 square grid has _____ border squares.

3. A 40 by 40 square grid has _____ border squares.

4. An N by N square grid has _____ border squares.

C. Find the missing parts.

1. A 4 by 8 square grid has _____ border squares.

2. A 6 by 15 square grid has _____ border squares.

3. A 20 by 60 square grid has _____ border squares.

4. An M by N square grid has _____ border squares.

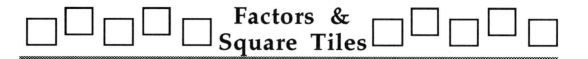

Use square tiles to form all possible rectangular arrays with the given number of squares. Record your results.

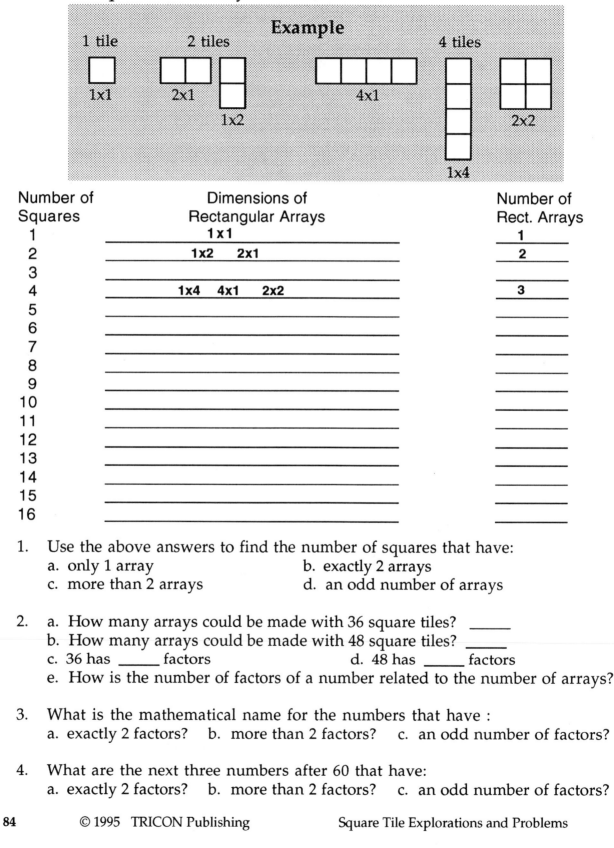

Number of Squares	Dimensions of Rectangular Arrays	Number of Rect. Arrays
1	**1 x 1**	**1**
2	**1x2 2x1**	**2**
3		
4	**1x4 4x1 2x2**	**3**
5		
6		
7		
8		
9		
10		
11		
12		
13		
14		
15		
16		

1. Use the above answers to find the number of squares that have:
   a. only 1 array
   b. exactly 2 arrays
   c. more than 2 arrays
   d. an odd number of arrays

2. a. How many arrays could be made with 36 square tiles? _____
   b. How many arrays could be made with 48 square tiles? _____
   c. 36 has _____ factors
   d. 48 has _____ factors
   e. How is the number of factors of a number related to the number of arrays?

3. What is the mathematical name for the numbers that have :
   a. exactly 2 factors?   b. more than 2 factors?   c. an odd number of factors?

4. What are the next three numbers after 60 that have:
   a. exactly 2 factors?   b. more than 2 factors?   c. an odd number of factors?

Use color tiles to build rectangles that satisfy all of the conditions stated in each of the below problems. Record your answers on the grid below.

1.
- 3 of my tiles are blue
- 3/4 of my tiles are red
- my perimeter is 14 units

2.
- 2 of my tiles are blue
- my perimeter is 16 units
- 5/6 of my tiles are red

3.
- 1/4 of my tiles are red
- 1/3 of my tiles are blue
- 1/6 of my tiles are yellow
- my perimeter is 20 units

4.
- 1/5 of my tiles are blue
- 1/2 of my tiles are yellow
- 1/10 of my tiles are red
- 5 of my tiles are green

5.
- 1/2 of my tiles are blue
- 1/5 of my tiles are yellow
- 1/10 of my tiles are green
- all other tiles are red
- my perimeter is 26 units

Use your square tiles to form a rectangle that satisfies all the conditions for each of the below problems. Sketch a solution.

1.   <u>Possible Solution</u>
* Perimeter equals 16 units
* 1/2 of the tiles are red
* 1/4 of the tiles are green
* 1/4 of the tiles are blue

2.
* Perimeter equals 14 units
* 1/3 of the tiles are red
* 1/2 of the tiles are green
* 1/6 of the tiles are blue

3.
* Perimeter equals 20 units
* 1/4 of the tiles are red
* 1/8 of the tiles are blue
* 1/2 of the tiles are green

4.
* Perimeter equals 18 units
* 20% of the tiles are yellow
* 25% of the tiles are red
* 30% of the tiles are blue
* 25% of the square tiles are green

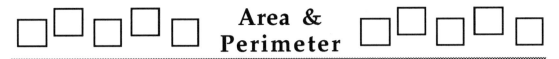
Determine whether each of the below rectangles can be formed. If possible, show how. If not possible, explain why not.

1. Can 24 square tiles be used to form a rectangle whose perimeter is:
   a. 20 units?   b. 25 units?

2. Can 16 square tiles be used to form a rectangle whose perimeter is:
   a. 20 units?   b. a perfect square?   c. a perfect cube?

3. Can 18 square tiles be used to form a rectangle whose perimeter is:
   a. 24 units?   b. 22 units

4. Can the square tiles be used to form a rectangle where, numerically:
   a. its area equals its perimeter?   b. its area is 4/5 of its perimeter?

5. Can the square tiles be used to form a rectangle where, numerically:
   a. its perimeter is one more than its area?
   b. its area is one more than its perimeter?

6. Can the square tiles be used to form a rectangle where, numerically:
   a. its area is two more than its perimeter?
   b. its area and perimeter are both odd numbers?

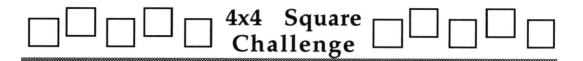

4x4 Square Challenge

The figure below shows how 9 colored tiles can form a 3x3 square so that each row and column contains a different color.

red	blue	green
green	red	blue
blue	green	red

Try to place 16 color tiles into the below 4x4 grid so that each row, column, and diagonal contains four different colors.

 Square Tile Explorations and Problems

Color Tiles
Clues

Materials: each group (2-4 students) - 6 red tiles, 6 blue tiles, 6 green tiles, 6 yellow tiles

Use the given clues to help you find the tiles I have.

1. **Clues:**
* I have 15 tiles
* I have no green tiles.
* I have one more red than blue.
* I have one more yellow than blue.

How many of my tiles are blue?

2. **Clues:**
* I have 13 tiles.
* All are either red, blue, or yellow.
* There are 3 more red than blue.
* There is one more blue than yellow.

How many of my tiles are red? blue? yellow?

3. **Clues:** (Devise a problem similar to those shown above.)

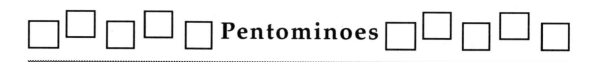
A pentomino (5-square pattern) can be formed by placing 5 square tiles so that each of the tiles has at least one complete side in common with another tile.

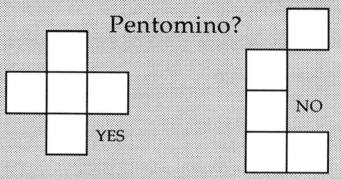

Pentomino?

YES   NO

1. Use your square tiles to find the 12 different pentominoes. Sketch each one below.
2. Find the 8 pentominoes that will fold into an open top box. Label the square (B) that would be the bottom of the box.
3. Find all line and rotational symmetries for each pentomino.

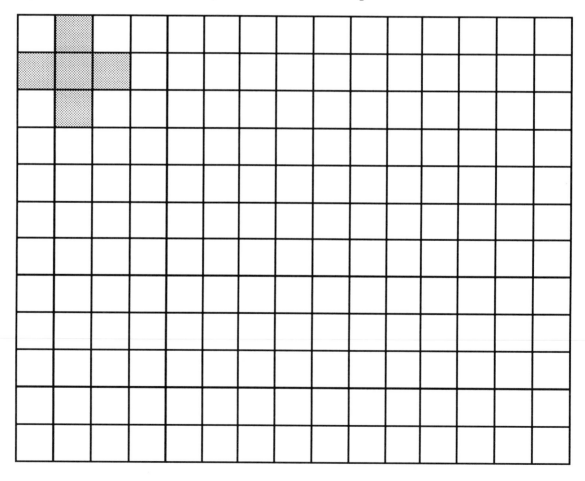

Place at least 5 tiles on squares in the first grid. Form a mirror image of that pattern by placing tiles on squares in the second grid.   The mirror is on the line shown.

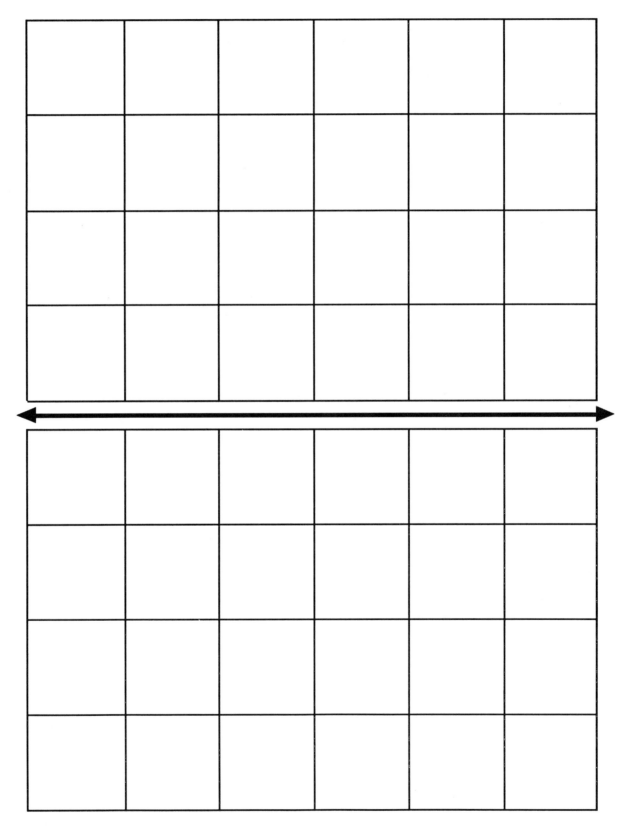

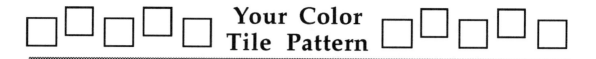
Materials: Color tiles and 1 playing board for each player.

Rules: 2-4 players each form a **color-tile-pattern** by placing a tile on all squares of their board.

Players then, in turn, display their **color-tile-pattern**.

All other players that discover the pattern score 1 point.

Players continue making patterns until one player scores 6 points and wins the game.

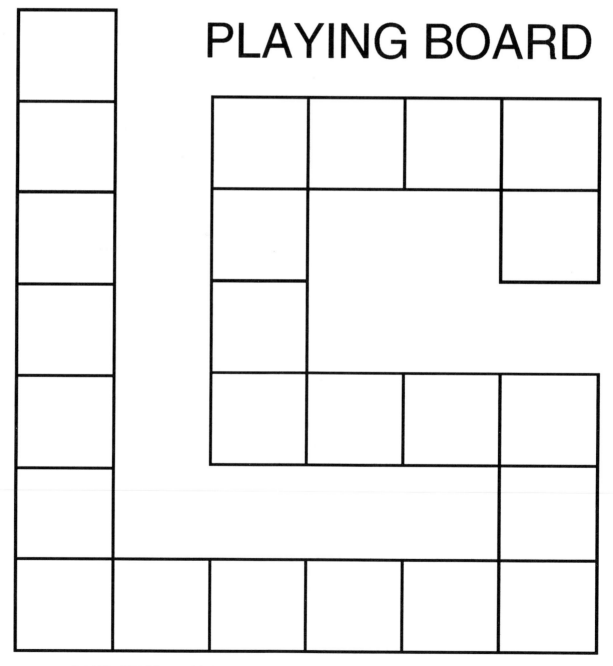

PLAYING BOARD

Your Color Tile Pattern

Materials: Color tiles and 1 playing board for each player.

Rules: 2-4 players each form a **color-tile-pattern** by placing a tile on all squares of their board.

Each player then removes all tiles that are not on their shaded squares.

Players then, in turn, display their **color-tile-pattern**.

Discover the pattern -- score 1 point.

Players continue making patterns until one player scores 5 points and wins the game.

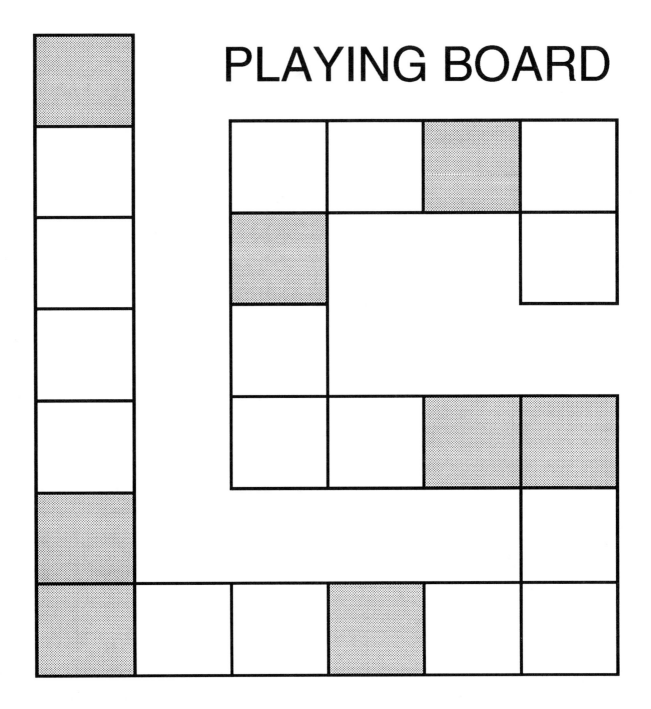

PLAYING BOARD

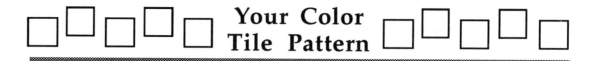
Try to form a color tile pattern by placing tiles on some of the empty squares. Then ask your classmates to guess your pattern in trying to find the color of the tile that could be in square A; in square B; in square C; in square D.

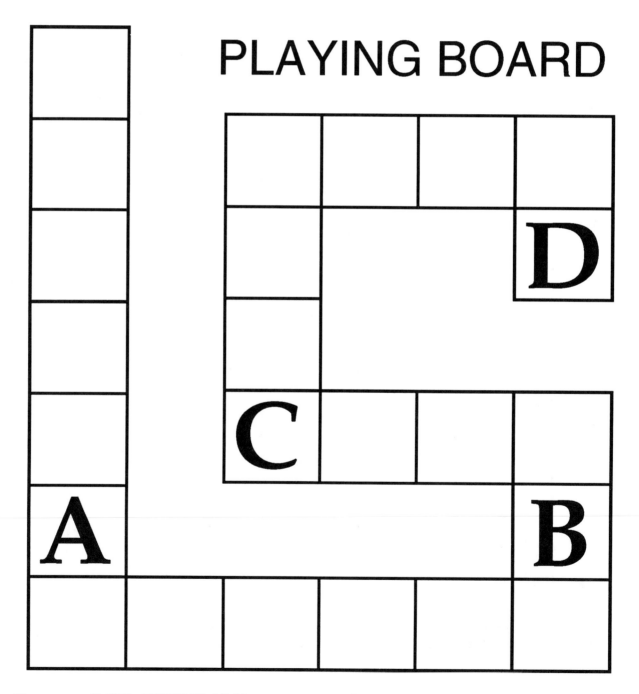

PLAYING BOARD

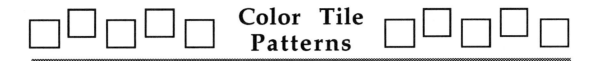

Try to find the missing tiles. B: Blue tile   R: Red tile

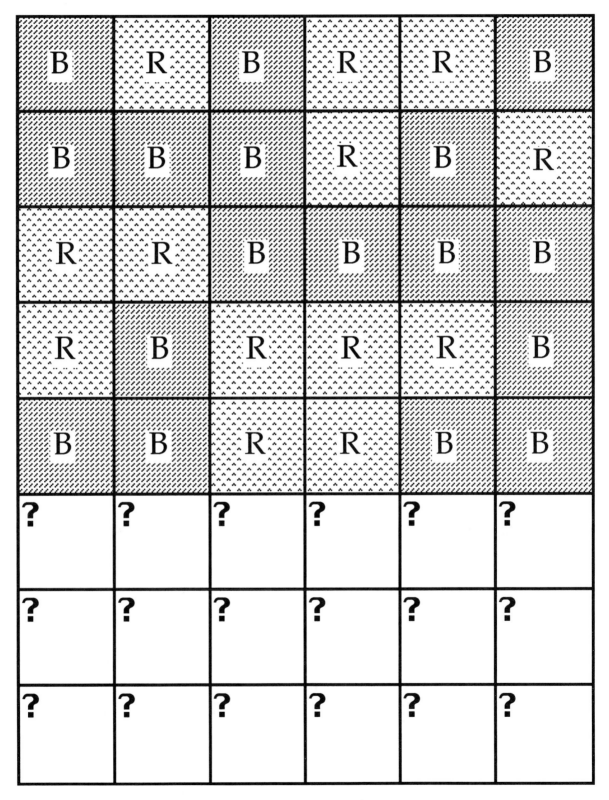

B	R	B	R	R	B
B	B	B	R	B	R
R	R	B	B	B	B
R	B	R	R	R	B
B	B	R	R	B	B
?	?	?	?	?	?
?	?	?	?	?	?
?	?	?	?	?	?

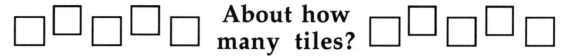

About how many tiles?

Devise a strategy and then use it to estimate how many square tiles would be needed:

1. to make a stack of tiles equal to your height?

2. to cover the floor in your math classroom?

3. to cover the land area of your state?

4. to fill your math classroom?

5. to make a line of tiles that is 1 mile long?
   1 kilometer long?

6. to balance 50 pounds on a balance scale? to balance
   50 kilograms?

          Square Tile Explorations and Problems

Place a square tile on each of the shaded squares. Then try to remove some of the tiles by using the following rules.

*A tile may jump an **adjacent** tile vertically, horizontally, or diagonally to one square beyond if that square is empty.

*Remove all of the "jumped" tiles.

*A series of two or more jumps is legal.

Your goal is to end up with only one tile.

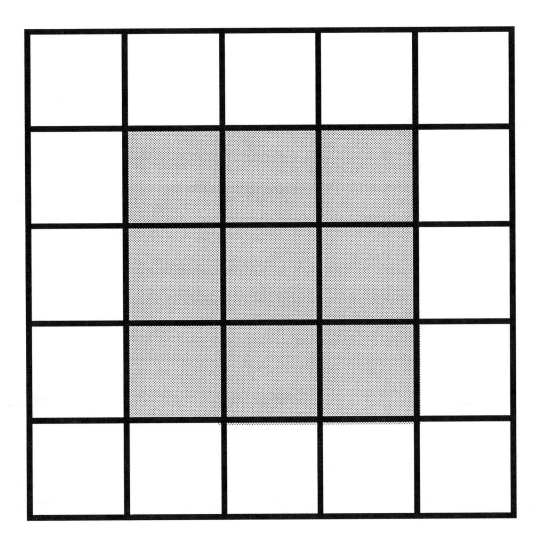

Make a "tower" using the numbered tiles (1-4) as shown below.
Goal: To move the tower from B to A or C in exactly 15 moves.
Rules:

   *Move one numbered tile at a time.
   *Always move the top numbered tile.
   *Always place the moved tile on the first open square (bottom to top).
   *The numbers on top must always be less than the numbers below.

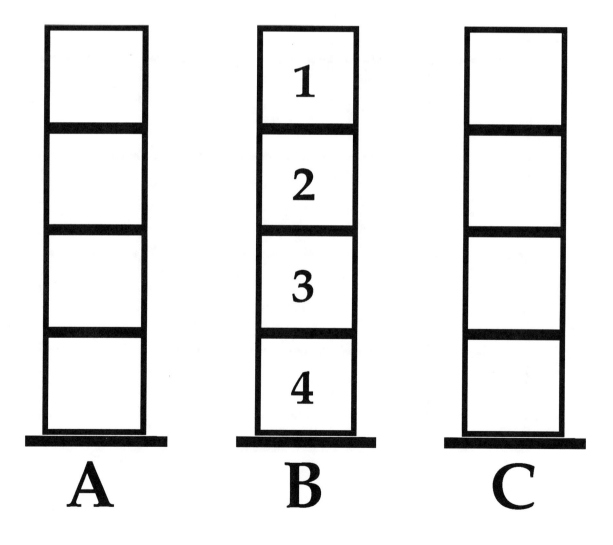

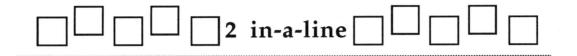

Try to place 12 square tiles on the below grid so that there are exactly two tiles in each row, column, and diagonal.

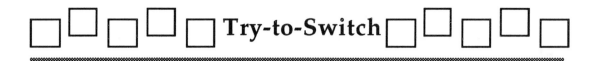

1. Place 3 tiles of one color in the squares labeled X and 3 tiles of another color on the squares labeled Y.

2. Try to switch the position of the tiles using the following rules:

   A. The X tiles must always move right and the Y tiles must always move left.
   B. Move one tile at a time to an empty square.
   C. A tile may jump a tile of another color into an empty space.
   D. Jumping a tile of the same color is not allowed.

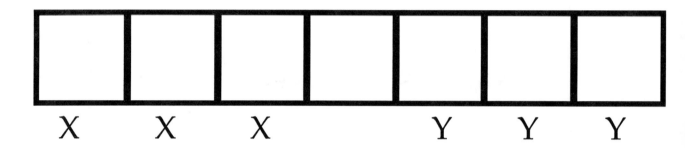

Complete the table shown below.

Number of tiles one color	Minimum number of moves to switch X and Y
1	———
2	———
3	———
4	———
5	———
.	
.	
.	
N	———

       Square Tile Explorations and Problems

RULES

* Place a square tile on each empty square.

* Two players take turns selecting either 1 tile, or 2 tiles that are next to each other.

* The player that picks up the last tile wins.

* Can the player that goes first be a sure winner? Explain.

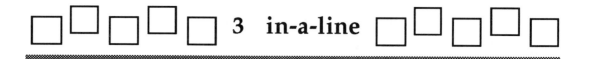

Materials: 3 color tiles for each player (2 different colors).

Rules:
Two players take turns placing their 3 tiles on a dot.
The center dot may not be used until all tiles are placed.
After all six tiles are on the board, the players continue by moving one of their tiles along a line to an adjacent uncovered dot.
The first player to get her/his three color tiles in-a-line horizontally, vertically, or diagonally wins the game.

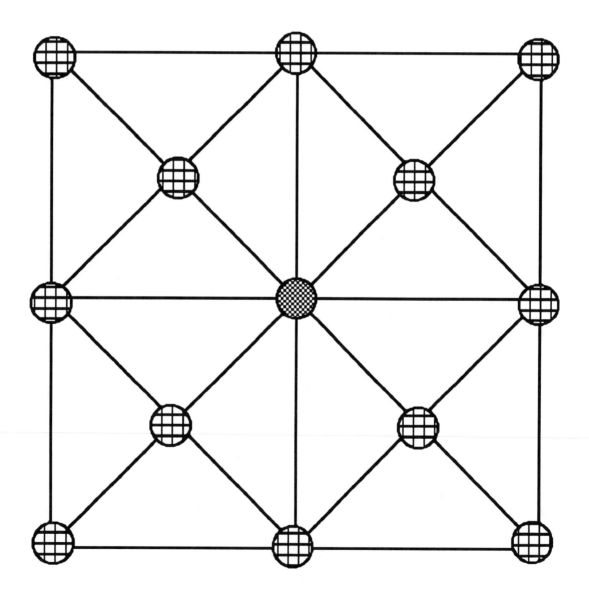

Game Rules

* Place 4 tiles in set A and 5 tiles in set B.
* Two players take turns removing either one tile from one of the sets or one tile from each of the sets A and B. The winner is the player that removes the last tile. Show how the first player can always win.

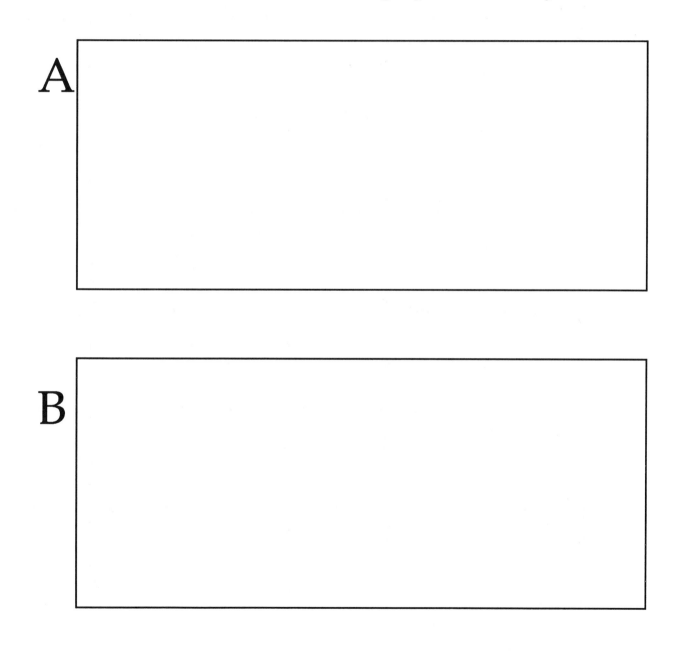

A

B

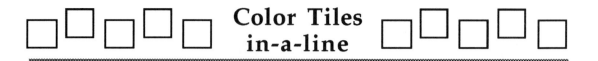

Color Tiles
in-a-line

Materials: 18 tiles of one color (A) and 18 color tiles of another color (B).

Rules: Two players (A) and (B) take turns placing their color tiles (1 per turn) until all 36 tiles are on the game board shown below. The player that ends up with the highest score wins.

Scoring: 3 in-a-line→3 points   4 in-a-line →4 points   5 in-a-line→5 points
All scoring is for Rows, Columns, and Diagonals.

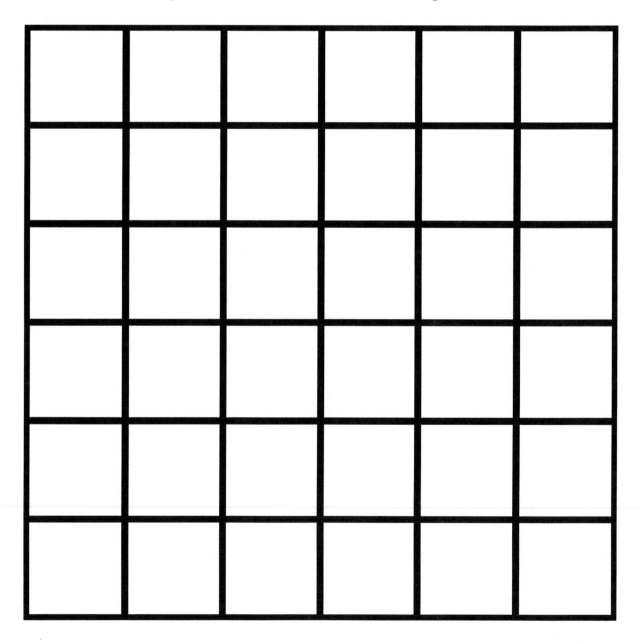

             Square Tile Explorations and Problems

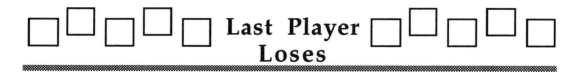
Start by covering the playing board with 25 tiles. Two players then take turns removing any number of <u>adjacent</u> tiles from any one row or column. Tiles may not be removed if there is a gap between them. The player that is forced to remove the last tile loses the game.

Game Board

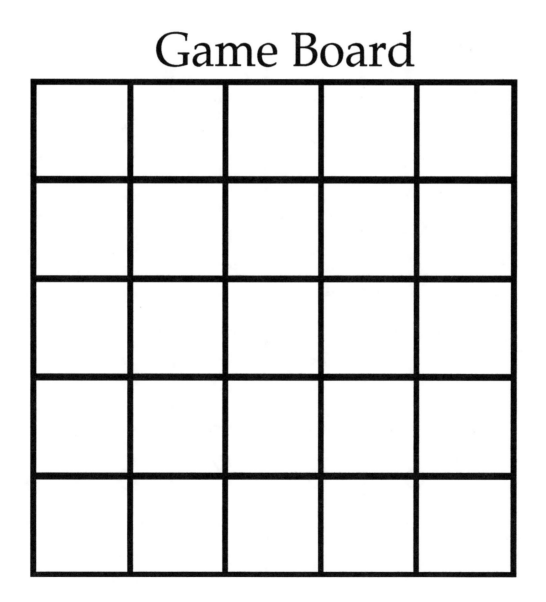

Dice Coverup

Materials: two dice, 24 square tiles (12 per player)

Rules: Two players (A & B) take turns tossing two dice. After each toss, a player puts one or more tiles on her/his board so that the numbers covered equal the total tossed. A round ends when each has had 6 tosses. Each player then finds the sum of her/his uncovered numbers. The one with the lowest total wins the round. The first player to win three rounds wins the game.

A

1	2	3	4
5	6	7	8
9	10	11	12

B

1	2	3	4
5	6	7	8
9	10	11	12

 Square Tile Explorations and Problems

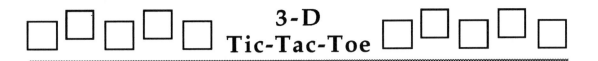
Materials: Red and blue square tiles

Rules:
Two players take turns placing their colored square tiles on the below 3 by 3 grid as follows:

On each turn a player puts a square tile of his/her color into an empty square or puts a tile on top of another tile already on the board if that square contains less than 3 tiles.

The winner is the first player to get 3 of his/her color in-a-line vertically, horizontally, diagonally, or 3 of his/her color on one square.

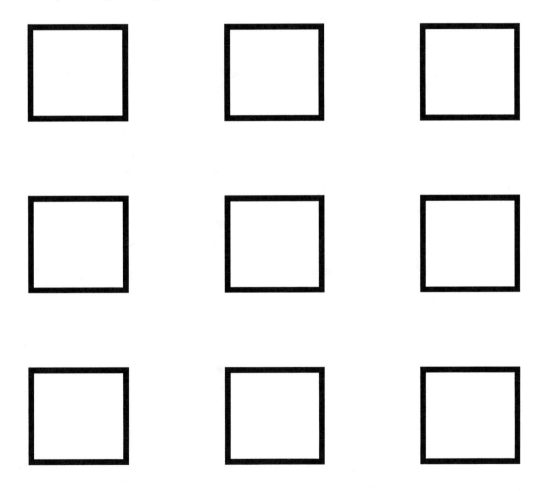

3-Player
Tic-Tac-Toe

Materials: red, blue, and yellow square tiles

Rules:
* Player #1: Place a red tile on an empty square.
* Player #2: Place a blue tile on an empty spuare.
* Player #3: Place a yellow tile on an empty square.
* The players continue taking turns in this way until someone gets 4 tiles of his/her color in any row, column, or diagonal. That player wins the game. If the board is completely covered with no 4 in-a-line of the same color, the game ends in a tie.

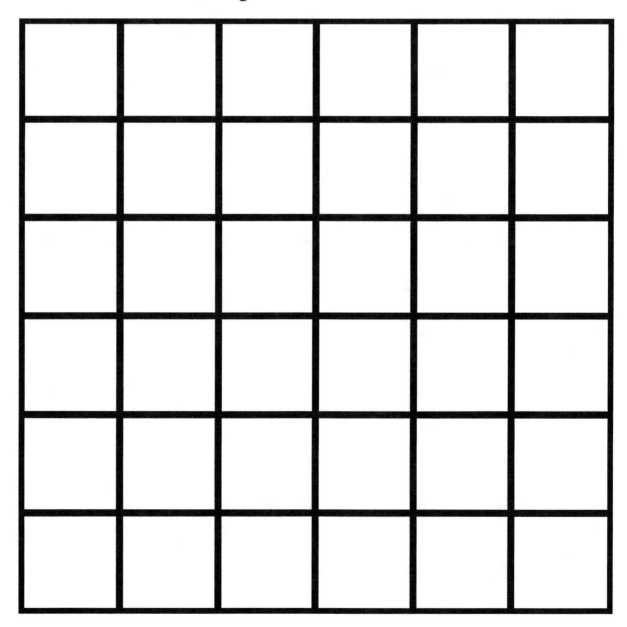

   Square Tile Explorations and Problems

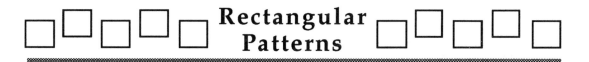

Rectangular Patterns

Cover the given rectangular array with 6 tiles of one color and 6 tiles of another color as shown. Can you continue the pattern in any direction?

After solving the problem, challenge your classmates by designing a similar rectangular pattern.

Page 1	Diagonals: 3, 5, 7; 4, 5, 6; 9, 5, 1; 8, 5, 2
Page 2	Left side: 4, 6, 8, 1 Bottom: 1, 9, 2, 7 Right Side: 7, 3, 5, 4 Sum = 19

Page 3
Sum = 23: Horizontally: 7, 9, 1, 2, 4   Vertically: 3, 8, 1, 6, 5
Sum = 24: Horizontally: 2, 9, 3, 6, 4   Vertically: 5, 8, 3, 7, 1
Sum = 25: Horizontally: 2, 8, 5, 7, 3   Vertically: 4, 9, 5, 6, 1
Sum = 26: Horizontally: 2, 8, 7, 6, 3   Vertically: 4, 9, 7, 5, 1

Page 4   Row 1: 2, 7, 6   Row 2: 9, 5 ,1   Row 3: 4, 3, 8

Page 6
1. Row 1: 6, 9   2. Row 1: 9, 6   3. Row 1: 3, 8
   Row 2: 3, 4   Row 2: 3, 5   Row 2: 7, 2

4. Row 1: 4, 6   5. Row 1: 3, 8   6. Row 1: 3, 9
   Row 2: 3, 7   Row 2: 6, 4   Row 2: 4, 2

Page 10
1. Row 1: 4, 8, 9   2. Row 1: 7, 8, 9   3. Row 1: 5, 4, 3
   Row 2: 6, 5, 2   Row 2: 6, 4, 2   Row 2: 1, 8, 9

Page 11
1. Row 1: 2, 7, 6   2. Row 1: 1, 9, 8   3. Row 1: 3, 6, 8
   Row 2: 5, 4, 8   Row 2: 7, 4, 3   Row 2: 5, 4, 7

Page 12
1. Row 1: 6, 7, 5   2. Row 1: 5, 9, 3   3. Row 1: 8, 1, 3
   Row 2: 3, 4, 8   Row 2: 4, 8, 7   Row 2: 6, 5, 9

Page 13
1. Row 1: 5, 6, 4   2. Row 1: 5, 8, 3   3. Row 1: 6, 3, 8
   Row 2: 7, 9, 2   Row 2: 9, 4, 6   Row 2: 2, 4, 1

Page 14
1. Row 1: 2, 6, 8   2. Row 1: 8, 9, 6   3. Row 1: 8, 4, 7
   Row 2: 9, 4, 3   Row 2: 4, 3, 2   Row 2: 3, 2, 5

Page 15
1. Row 1: 3, 5, 4   2. Row 1: 2, 3, 7   3. Row 1: 7, 6, 4
   Row 2: 7, 6, 8   Row 2: 4, 5, 1   Row 2: 5, 8, 9

Page 16
A. Row 1: 2, 3, 6   B. Row 1: 1, 3, 5
   Row 2: 4, 5, 1   Row 2: 6, 7, 9
   Row 3: 8, 7, 9   Row 3: 4, 8, 2

Page 17
A. Row 1: 1, 9, 6   B. Row 1: 7, 5, 2
   Row 2: 8, 5, 4   Row 2: 3, 1, 9
   Row 3: 7, 3, 2   Row 3: 8, 6, 4

Page 18
A. Row 1: 5, 2, 3   B. Row 1: 6, 2, 3
   Row 2: 6, 1, 4   Row 2: 1, 9, 7
   Row 3: 7, 8, 9   Row 3: 8, 4, 5

Page 19	A. Row 1: 8, 7, 5 Row 2: 9, 6, 4	B. Row 1: 3, 7, 9 Row 2: 4, 8, 2	

Page 20	A. Row 1: 2, 9, 3 Row 2: 4, 6, 1	B. Row 1: 4, 8, 2 Row 2: 3, 7, 9	

Page 21
1. $5x8-2=38$ $6x4-3=21$
2. $8x9-2=70$ $4x6+5=29$
3. $8x9-1=71$ $6x7+2=44$
4. $1x4x9=36$ $6(7-2)=30$
5. $5x9+2=47$ $4x6-1=23$
6. $1+3+8=12$ $4(6+9)=60$
7. $3+6+8=17$ $5(7-1)=30$
8. $3+8+9=20$ $4x5+1=21$
9. $6x9-7=47$ $4x5+1=21$

Page 22
1. Row 1: 4, 5, 3
   Row 2: 8, 9, 1
   Row 3: 6, 2, 7
2. Row 1: 1, 9, 3
   Row 2: 2, 5, 4
   Row 3: 6, 8, 7

Page 23
1. Row 1: 4, 3, 5
   Row 2: 9, 2, 1
   Row 3: 8, 7, 6
2. Row 1: 3, 4, 5
   Row 2: 2, 8, 7
   Row 3: 6, 9, 1

Page 24
1. Row 1: 2, 4, 7
   Row 2: 3, 8, 1
   Row 3: 6, 5, 9
2. Row 1: 1, 8, 5
   Row 2: 2, 7, 6
   Row 3: 3, 9, 4

Page 25
1. Row 1: 9, 5, 3
   Row 2: 6, 8, 1
   Row 3: 7, 4, 2
2. Row 1: 7, 4, 2
   Row 2: 9, 5, 6
   Row 3: 3, 8, 1

Page 26
1. Row 1: 8, 4, 5
   Row 2: 7, 3, 2
   Row 3: 1, 6, 9
2. Row 1: 8, 6, 3
   Row 2: 7, 2, 1
   Row 3: 5, 9, 4

Page 27
1. Row 1: 6, 3, 1
   Row 2: 9, 4, 2
   Row 3: 7, 5, 8
2. Row 1: 2, 3, 8
   Row 2: 9, 1, 6
   Row 3: 4, 5, 7

Page 28
1. $3x7-1=20$ (A) $4(8+2)=40$ (B) $5x6+9=39$ (C)
2. $8(5-4)=8$ (A) $6(3+7)=60$ (B) $1x2x9=18$ (C)
3. $5x8+7=47$ (A) $4(1+3)=16$ (B) $6+9-2=13$ (C)
4. $5x4+1=21$ (A) $8x3-9=15$ (B) $7x6+2=44$ (C)
5. $1x3x4=12$ (A) $6(7-5)=12$ (B) $2x9+8=26$ (C)

Page 29
1. $6(1+7)=48$ $4+8-5=7$ $3(2+9)=33$
2. $2x9-8=10$ $5x6-1=29$ $4x7-3=25$
3. $9(3-1)=18$ $2x5x7=70$ $4(8-6)=8$
4. $5x6-3=27$ $8(2+4)=48$ $7(1+9)=70$
5. $5(9-7)=10$ $3x6-8=10$ $1x2x4=8$

Page 30
1. 2+3+5=10
2. 3x7+8=29
3. 2+7+9=18
4. 5x9-2=43
5. 3(1+5)=18

7x6+4=46
6x9-1=53
3x6+1=19
6+7-8=5
4x6+8=32

8(1+9)=80
4x5-2=18
4x8-5=27
4(1+3)=16
9(2+7)=81

Page 31
1. 3x7+2=23
2. 4(6+5)=44
3. 4x6+3=27
4. 4(1+9)=40
5. 1x3x6=18

4x5-9=11
7(9-3)=42
1x5x7=35
5(6-3)=15
5(4-2)=10

6x8-1=47
2x8+1=17
2+8+9=19
8+7+2=17
8(9-7)=16

Page 32
Row 1: 4,6,8

Row 2: 7,9,2

Row 3: 5,1,3

Page 33
B. Row 1: 3, 4, 7
   Row 2: 2, 9, 1
   Row 2: 5, 6, 8

C. Row 1: 3, 7, 1
   Row 2: 2, 9, 8
   Row 2: 5, 4, 6

D. Row 1: 3, 9, 5
   Row 2: 7, 8, 4
   Row 2: 6, 2, 1

Page 34
1. Row 1: 8, 2, 9
   Row 2: 5, 4, 1
   Row 3: 6, 3, 7

2. Row 1: 6, 3, 7
   Row 2: 5, 4, 1
   Row 3: 8, 9, 2

Page 35
1. Row 1: 3, 7, 4
   Row 2: 8, 6, 5
   Row 3: 1, 2, 9

2. Row 1: 6, 2, 7
   Row 2: 9, 4, 3
   Row 3: 5, 8, 1

Page 36
1. Row 1: 8,2,1
   Row 2: 4,9,3
   Row 3: 5,7,6

2. Row 1: 9,2,1
   Row 2: 3,8,5
   Row 3: 4,6,7

Page 37
1. Row 1: 6, 2, 8
   Row 2: 3, 4, 9
   Row 3: 5, 1, 7

2. Row 1: 3, 7, 9
   Row 2: 6, 5, 1
   Row 3: 2, 8, 4

Page 51
1. (2x7+1)÷3=5
4. 9÷3+7-6=4
7. 9÷3+8-6=5
10. 3+8÷2-1=6
13. (1+3+6)÷2=5

2. 2x8-7x1=9
5. 8-1x7+5=6
8. 8+6-3x4=2
11. (8+7)÷3+4=9
14. 2x9-3x4=6

3. 3x4-6÷2=9
6. (8+1)÷3+4=7
9. (1x7+5)÷2=6
12. 8÷2+9÷3=7

Square Tile Explorations and Problems

Page 53

a. 2768
    + 345
    3113

b. 6327
    + 845
    7172

c. 2897
    + 564
    3461

d. 3619
    + 578
    4197

e. 8963
    + 241
    9204

f. 4125
    + 936
    5061

g. 6789
    + 524
    7313

h. 2937
    + 416
    3353

i. 7489
    + 563
    8052

Page 54

a. 291
    + 56
    347

b. 591
    + 47
    638

c. 587
    + 34
    621

d. 468
    + 71
    539

e. 479
    + 82
    561

f. 378
    + 51
    429

g. 496
    + 31
    527

h. 524
    + 93
    617

Page 55

a. 6389
    - 715
    5674

b. 1756
    - 934
    822

c. 4126
    - 859
    3267

d. 2586
    - 914
    1672

e. 9253
    - 184
    9069

f. 4196
    - 823
    3373

g. 1234
    - 567
    667

h. 5968
    - 132
    5836

i. 7683
    - 541
    7142

Page 56

a. 621
    - 534
    87

b. 631
    - 582
    49

c. 621
    - 573
    48

d. 621
    - 543
    78

e. 921
    - 876
    45

f. 612
    - 538
    74

g. 731
    - 649
    82

h. 527
    - 491
    36

Page 57

1. 491
    + 36
    527

2. 427
    - 58
    369

3. 49
    28
    + 76
    153

4. 218
    + 736
    954

Page 58   1. 21402=369x58   2. 258=356-98   3. 1039=986+53

4. 12596=268x57   5. 2.83≈246÷87   6. 953=965-12

7. 4108=158x26   8. 137=234-97   9. 445=356+89

Page 59   Missing digits by row are: 7; 3; 2, 8; 4, 5; 1, 9; 6

Page 60   Missing digits by row are: 3; 5; 1; 4, 2; 9; 7; 6; 8

Page 61   a. 6x45=270   b. 8x61=488   c. 6x48=288
             8x37=296   2x94=188   7x23=161

d. 8x23=184   e. 4x58=232   f. 5x64=320
   4x67=268   2x73=146   7x32=224

g. 8x62=496   h. 8x19=152   i. 7x54=378
   3x94=282   6x27=162   8x29=232

Page 62.   a. 4x65=260   b. 5x96=480   c. 6x38=288
              3x28=84   4x32=128   7x24=168
              7x19=133   7x18=126   9x51=459

d. 9x18=162   e. 4x51=204   f. 8x52=416
   5x43=215   7x32=224   9x17=153
   6x72=432   8x69=552   4x36=144

Page 63   a. 3x87=261   c. 5x28=140
              6x19=114   4x93=372
              5x42=210   6x17=102

Page 64   1.
x	51	78
32		
69		

2.
x	42	57
39		
68		

Page 65   1.
x	46	58
31		
79		

2.
x	52	49
87		
36		

Page 67   5x78+23=413   8x39-56=256   6x49+75=369
           4x86-51=293   9x73+65=722   6x58-29=319

Page 70   1. 1,3,5,2 (A,B,C,D)   2. 3,2,4,6   3. 3,6,9,5
           4. 3,4,6,8   5. 2,4,5,6   6. 2,3,5,4
           7. 1,2,4,9   8. 6,3,5,7   9. 1,8,2,5
           10. 8,1,3,6

Page 71	Row 1: 2,1,6	Row 2: 3,5,8	

Page 72

1. 5	2. 6	3. 1	
4. 28	5. 7	6. 3	7. 49

Page 73 Possible solutions:

1. 1,2,4 8,9 2. 1,3 2,4,5,7 6,8 3. 1 2,3,4
4. 1,5,9 2,6,7 3,4,8 5. 2,3,8 6. 1,4,9
7. 1,6,9 8. 9 1,2,5,8 9. 1,2,3,6
10. 4,7

Page 74 Possible solutions

1. A 7,9	B 1,3,4,5,6	2. A 2,3,4,6	B 5,9
3. A 2,3,4,6	B 1,5,9	4. A 6,9	B 1,2,3,5,7
5. A 1,6	B 2,3	6. A 1,6	B 2,3,4,8

Page 75

1. A 4,5	B 7,9	C 4,6,7,8	2. A 1,4,5	B 2,9	C 2,4,6
3. A 1,3,5	B 2,7	C 2,3,4,6,8	4. A 3,4,6	B 5,8	C 2,3,8
5 A 2,3,6	B 1,4,5	C 1,3,9			

Page 76

1. A 2,6,9	B 1,2,3,5,6,7	2. A 2,9	B 4,5,7,9
3. A 1,9	B 1,2,4,8	4. A 6,9	B 1,2,4,5,6
5. A 2,4	B 1,3,8	6. A 1,2,4,7	B 2,5,6

Page 78

1. a. 8 {R B Y RB RY BY RBY Empty Set} b. 16

2. 2, 4, 8, 16, 32, 2^{11} 3. 2^N

Page 79

1. True	2. True (2x2)	3. False	4. True
5. False (4x4)	6. True (1x17)	7. False (28)	8. True

Page 81

A. Square Tables	#2 13	#3 16		
No. of People	28	34		
B. Square Tables	#4 19	#5 22	#20 67	#N 3N+7
C. No. of People	40	46	136	2N+2

Page 82

Rectangle	**# Tiles to surround**	**Perimeter**
N x N	4N + 4	4N + 8
M x N	2M + 2N + 4	2M + 2N + 8

Page 83

B.	1. 20	2. 36	3. 156	4. 4N - 4
C.	1. 20	2. 38	3. 156	4. 2M + 2N - 4

Page 84

1. a. 1 b. 2, 3, 5, 7, 11, 13
c. 4, 6, 8, 9, 10, 12, 14, 15, 16 d. 1, 4, 9, 16
2. a. 9 b. 10 c. 9 d.10 e. Same
3. a. Primes b. Composites c. Perfect squares

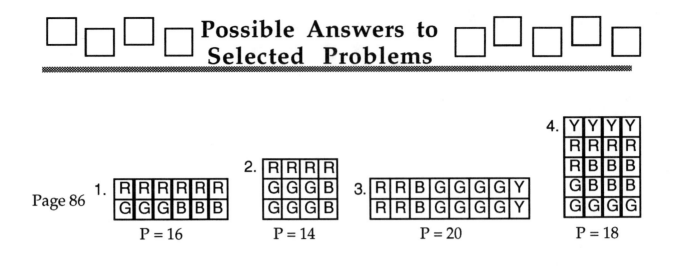

Page 86   1. R R R R R R / G G G B B B   P = 16

2. R R R R / G G G B / G G G B   P = 14

3. R R B G G G G Y / R R B G G G G Y   P = 20

4. Y Y Y Y / R R R R / R B B B / G B B B / G G G G   P = 18

Page 99

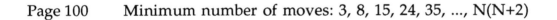

Page 100   Minimum number of moves: 3, 8, 15, 24, 35, ..., N(N+2)